Computing
is Easy

COMPUTING IS EASY

David Parker and
Martin Hann

Newnes Technical Books

Newnes Technical Books

is an imprint of the Butterworth Group
which has principal offices in
London, Boston, Durban, Singapore, Sydney, Toronto, Wellington

First published 1982
Reprinted 1983

© **Butterworth & Co. (Publishers) Ltd, 1982**

Every effort has been made to ensure that this book can be used with all
of the popular microcomputers supporting Microsoft Basic. However,
neither the authors nor the publishers are able to guarantee that all of
the programs and text will be applicable to all machines due to the
increasing number of new microcomputers coming onto the market.

British Library Cataloguing in Publication Data

Parker, David
  Computing is easy
  1. Microcomputers — Juvenile literature
  I. Title   II. Hann, Martin
  001.64'04   QA76.5

  ISBN 0-408-01203 X

Typeset by Tunbridge Wells Typesetting Services Ltd
Printed in England by Butler and Tanner Ltd., Frome and London

Preface

This book is intended primarily for the fast-growing band of children who have access to personal microcomputers at home or school, and who wish to gain the knowledge necessary to participate actively in the computer revolution; knowledge that will stand them in excellent stead in the years to come as our society relies more and more on high technology, and on computers in particular.

The book introduces beginners to the computer and encourages them to explore its capabilities by means of carefully prepared programs and experiments using the BASIC programming language. At the end of the book they will be writing their own programs and have a good working knowledge of the computer. They will then be prepared (and, we hope, keen!) to progress to more advanced operations to be found in other publications.

The authors gratefully acknowledge the assistance of several people in the preparation of this book: Diane who typed the manuscript; Helen who thought up the cartoons; Philip for helping to write the programs; both of our wives for their forbearance; and Dartmouth College for inventing 'BASIC' in the first place.

D.P.
M.H.

Contents

Introduction

If you asked us 'What is a computer?', we would tell you that it is a box filled with electric wires, transistors and things. If you asked us how it worked, we would reply with blank faces. We don't know how computers work. Fortunately, we don't need to know. Many people drive cars without knowing how they work. What they do know is how to use cars — how to drive them. What this book will do is teach you how to *use* a computer. It will teach you how to 'talk' to a computer in a way that both you and the computer understand so that you can make the computer *work* for you.

To use this book you will need to have the use of a computer of some sort. Hopefully, you have one at home, or perhaps there is one at your school which you can use.

Once you know how to operate the computer you will be able to do the experiments in this book by yourself and you will teach yourself as you go along. You may however need someone who knows how to operate the computer to show you how to switch on etc., and whom you can ask for advice if you get stuck.

In a few years time we shall probably be able to talk to computers like we talk to our friends at school and the computers will tell us the answers to our problems by talking back to us. At the moment we can't do that so we have to have some other method of 'communicating' with the computer. To give information (or 'data') to a computer we use a keyboard. Usually this is joined on to the front of the computer, rather like the keys on a calculator are part of the actual calculator. The keys of the computer look like those of a typewriter — in fact most of the letters and numbers are in the same place as they are on a typewriter. The computer knows what all these keys are so can easily understand us when we give it instructions by typing them in on the keyboard.

So we have our computer and we can talk to it by typing instructions and data on the keyboard. Now all we need is some way for the computer to talk back to us. For this, we use a video screen. This screen may be one made specially for the computer, or we may be using a computer at home plugged in to an ordinary television set. It doesn't make any difference which one is used.

Now we are ready to go; we have a computer, we can 'talk' to it by using the keyboard, and it can 'talk' back to us by using the video screen. There are just three things to remember before you start:

Firstly, there are certain ways in which some computers work differently from others. For instance, the key at the right-hand end of the keyboard which you press when you have finished typing a line is usually labelled 'RETURN', but on some computers it is called 'NEWLINE', or even 'ENTER'.

Also in this book we shall be asking you to type words into your computer such as PRINT and LIST. These words are called 'key words' and you may find that the computer you are using has keys marked with them, in which case you need only press the appropriate key. If your computer does not have such keys, you will have to spell the words out by typing their individual letters. You may also find that to type certain characters, for example the plus sign (+), the asterisk (*) or quotation marks (''), you may need to press the 'SHIFT' key at the same time. There may be several other little differences like this, but they shouldn't cause any real difficulty.

Secondly, we shall sometimes be asking you to switch off your computer. With most computers it is perfectly in order just to switch off, but with others it is important that the switching-off instructions in the computers' manuals are followed, especially for systems with disk drives, or ones in which the 'BASIC' operating language has to be loaded into the computer from a cassette tape.

Finally, always remember that whatever you type in you cannot do the computer any damage, so don't be afraid to experiment. Type something in to see if it works. If it doesn't, you can always try again. As you go through the book we shall give you programs and experiments to try, but you should also try to make our programs better and to make up other programs of your own.

1

Your computer as a calculator

We've all used small electronic calculators. They are really small computers. But they only do one calculation at a time.

Computers do calculations just like calculators.

Try this: switch on the computer and get it ready to use as described in the manual supplied with it. Now type in

PRINT 22 + 33

and press the RETURN key. (Remember it might be called NEWLINE or ENTER.)

The computer now 'PRINTs' on the screen the answer

55

and that is exactly the sort of calculation that a pocket calculator will do. That sort of calculation on a computer is called an 'Immediate Mode' calculation as it is done immediately. 'PRINT 22 + 33' is an instruction to the computer which in future we shall call a 'statement'.

The computer can also multiply, divide or take away just as a calculator can and we'll now try a few calculations.

There are a few differences in the signs that we use when instructing the computer. The add (+) and take away (−) signs are the same but instead of × for times we use the asterisk (*) and instead of ÷ for divide we use the slash (/).

So here are a few statements for you to try:

    PRINT 43 + 43
    PRINT 2 * 12
    PRINT 4 * 15
    PRINT 15 / 3
    PRINT 28 / 7
    PRINT 15 − 7
    PRINT 98 − 42

Press RETURN after each statement and the computer will give you the answer.

Now try some more of your own — you could check that the answers are correct by doing the same calculations on a calculator, if one is available.

Certain computers only work in whole numbers so if you were to divide 9 by 5 the answer may be shown as 1 when it should be 1·8. The reason for this is explained in Chapter 12. If your computer is one of these, you can still do everything in this book but you should remember that some answers will not be absolutely exact!

The most important difference between a calculator and a computer is that the computer can *remember* lots of things you tell it and can use the information it has remembered to do all sorts of complicated things. If you give the computer a list of statements to perform, that list is called a COMPUTER PROGRAM. The computer will perform or 'execute' all the statements one after the other — but only when you tell it to do so. It will then be acting in 'deferred' mode as it puts off, or 'defers', executing them until you tell it to. By remembering lots of statements (the program) and waiting for all of them before it does anything, the computer can do many more difficult and complicated things than a calculator.

In every-day life you often need to use more than one instruction to do a particular job. For example, if a friend asks you the way to the local swimming pool, you usually need to give him several instructions such as, 'Turn left at the traffic lights, take the second turning on the right, go past the park and the swimming pool is on your left.' This is a sort of program. He has to do the first instruction first, and only when he's done that can he do the second instruction and then the third. He is a bit like a computer — he waits until you have given him *all* your instructions, he remembers them, then he

performs them one after the other. If he were like a calculator you would only be able to give him one instruction at a time and you would have to run after him and give him the next one when he came to the next turning. Much easier for you if he is like a computer!

As well as remembering programs, your computer can also remember lots of other information. It can remember numbers, such as the ages of everyone in your school, or words, such as all their names, or numbers and letters, such as car number plates.

As you go through this book we will show you how to get the computer to remember all sorts of different things and then use the information to do many clever and interesting things.

2

Numeric variables and the LET statement

In this chapter we shall look at how your computer remembers numbers and how you can get it to use those numbers.

The computer's memory is like lots and lots of separate little boxes, or cells, which you can think of as being rather like the honeycomb inside a beehive. Each little box has a label — let's call the boxes Box A, Box B, Box C, etc., as in this diagram:

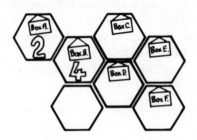

You could put any numbers you like into these boxes. In the diagram you will see that Box A has a 2 in it, Box B has a 4 in it. To find out what your computer has in its own boxes A and B, type:

    PRINT A (press RETURN)

then type

    PRINT B (press RETURN)

In each case you probably got the answer Ø (zero), showing you that there is nothing in these boxes yet. (The computer you are using may not PRINT anything at all if the value is zero.)

Now type:

    LET A = 2 (press RETURN)
    LET B = 4 (press RETURN)

You have just told the computer to put 2 into its Box A and 4 into its Box B. To make sure that it has done this, type:

PRINT A (press RETURN)
PRINT B (press RETURN)

The computer should have replied 2 and then 4, showing that these are the values that it has actually put into these boxes.

The computer will remember these numbers for as long as you like provided you do not switch it off. If you were to switch off, then on again, you would find that the numbers in all the memory boxes have changed back to zeros, so keep the computer switched on until you have finished this chapter.

Now, if you told the computer that its Box C was to equal A + B, what would you expect its Box C to contain? Let's try it. Type:

LET C = A + B (press RETURN)
PRINT C (press RETURN)

Is the answer what you expected? It should be 6, which is the number in Box A plus the number in Box B.

Now tell the computer that its Box D is to equal Box B take away Box A. To do this, type in:

LET D = B−A (press RETURN)
PRINT D (press RETURN)

The computer should PRINT the answer 2, which is 4 minus 2. So Box D now has 2 in it.

Now check the values in each of the computer's boxes. Type:

PRINT A
PRINT B
PRINT C
PRINT D
PRINT E
(Press RETURN after each line.)

5

What is the value of E? It is still zero because you have not yet told the computer to put anything in that box.

Let's give E the value of all the other boxes added together. Type:

LET E = A + B + C + D
PRINT E
(Press RETURN after each line.)

The computer should display (or PRINT) on the screen the value of E which is now 2 + 4 + 6 + 2 which is 14.

These boxes A, B, C, etc. are called VARIABLES because you can vary the numbers put into them. You wouldn't call the number 7 a variable because it can only be a 7 and will be for the rest of its life! The variable A in a computer though can be any number you want it to be, and so it is called a NUMERIC VARIABLE.

When you first switched on your computer, each of the boxes had Ø, or nothing, in it but now you have put different numbers into all these boxes. Remember, if you turn your computer off now, it will forget all these numbers. You could check that by switching off, then on again, and typing PRINT and a box number. (Remember our warning in the Introduction about switching off certain computers.)

Here is something for you to try. Type:

LET A = 5
LET B = 3
LET C = B + B
LET D = C / 3
LET E = D − 5
LET F = A * B
(Press RETURN after each line as usual)

Now write in these boxes what you think the values of A, B, C, D, E and F will be:

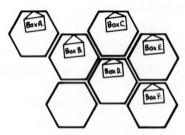

Do you know how to check? Of course you do! Type:

PRINT A
PRINT B
and so on and the computer will tell you!

Up to now we have dealt with two words that the computer understands — PRINT and LET. These are just two keywords which we can use to instruct the computer but we shall be covering many more as we go through this book. A computer is only able to understand instructions written using keywords. You cannot do any damage by trying to instruct the computer in words it does not know, but your programs will not work — the computer will just tell you that you have made an error.

In the next chapter we shall type a program into our computer and find out if it is as clever as it thinks it is! Up to now, we have been telling the computer to do one calculation at a time such as PRINT A + B or PRINT B−A. You will remember that this is called working in 'immediate' mode as each calculation is done immediately. In Chapter 3 we shall put several statements into the computer and tell it to wait until it has all of them before doing anything. This is called 'deferred' mode. Remember the person who wanted to know the way to the swimming pool? Chapter 3 is the chapter when we meet a real live computer program!

3

More statements and simple editing

We shall now give the computer a program to execute. The first thing to do whenever you are going to put a program into your computer is to make sure that there is nothing left in its memory that will muck up your program. To do this we type NEW and press RETURN. This clears everything out of the computer ready for your nice new program to go in. If you wish, you can check that Boxes A, B and C, etc., which we met in the last chapter, have values of zero after you typed NEW. (You know how to do this, remember?)

Now type in the program below. If you make a mistake when typing a statement line, don't worry! You can just type the line number (the number at the beginning of the line) and the statement again, and the computer will only take notice of the last thing you typed by any line number. Alternatively, you can use the DEL, DELETE, RUBOUT or the ← key to move the cursor back along the line so you can correct any mistakes without having to retype the whole line.

```
1 LET A = 5
2 LET B = 3
3 LET C = B + B
4 LET D = C / 3
5 LET E = D - 5
6 LET F = A * B
7 END (or STOP)
```

You may have noticed that these lines are the same as the statements you typed in towards the end of the last chapter. This time though, we have numbered all the lines. Line numbers tell the computer that it is to act in deferred mode — when it sees line numbers, the computer knows it must wait until you tell it before acting on any statements. Also, you will see that we have finished off the program with an END statement. (Some computers use the word STOP.) When you tell the computer to do so, it will look at the line with the lowest number and do whatever it says, then it will look at the next highest number and do that, and so on. The command to tell the computer that it can go ahead and actually do that is RUN.

Now type RUN, and press RETURN. Nothing very exciting appeared to happen, but if you now check the values of A, B, C, D, E and F, you will find that they have the same values as they did when you filled in the boxes in the last chapter.

Don't turn off the computer or type NEW or anything, just type these extra lines:

```
 7 PRINT A
 8 PRINT B
 9 PRINT C
10 PRINT D
11 PRINT E
12 PRINT F
13 END
```

If you now type LIST and press RETURN, the computer will list on the screen your whole program. You will notice that line 7 has changed from END to PRINT A. This is because, as we said just now, the computer only remembers the last thing you type by a particular line number.

If you now type RUN and press RETURN the computer will do the following:

First — it sees RUN and changes all the variables back to zero ready for the new program it is expecting.

Second —it performs or 'executes' each line of the program in order, just as it did before. So it sets up all the variables, A,

B, etc. and does the sums you have told it to in line numbers 1 to 6. Then it PRINTs all the variables as you have told it to in lines 7 to 12.

Third — when it sees line 13 with END written in it, it tells you that it has finished RUNning that program and that it is waiting for new instructions. It may say 'READY' or 'OK' or something similar.

When you ran your program, the computer should have displayed the following results on the screen:

```
   5
   3
   6
   2
  -3
  15
```

Is this what happened? If not, you have probably made a typing error. Type LIST and press RETURN and check carefully that everything is correctly typed.

Computers do calculations very, very quickly. So quickly, in fact, that the answer is displayed on the screen almost before you have taken your finger off the RETURN key; but the computer actually did all the things we said it would when RUNning your program.

In Chapter 4 we shall continue with this program. If you are going to read Chapter 4 straight away, do not switch off your computer — this will save you having to retype your program.

4

PRINT layout

If you have not switched off your computer since the end of the last chapter, your program will still be in the computer's memory. If you did switch off, you must now type the program again and RUN it to make sure it works.

Up to now, we have PRINTed each answer on a separate line like this:

```
   5
   3
   6
   2
  −3
  15
```

Now type LIST and change lines 7 to 12 so that they look like this (don't forget the commas):

```
 7 PRINT A,
 8 PRINT B,
 9 PRINT C,
1Ø PRINT D,
11 PRINT E,
12 PRINT F,
```

Remember that to change lines you can just type the lines again. The newly-typed lines are the only ones remembered: prove it by typing LIST.

Notice the commas at the end of lines 7 to 12. Now type RUN.

The results of this will differ from computer to computer but what will have happened is that more than one number will have been PRINTed on a line. Perhaps nearly all of them are on one line. This is because the comma causes each new variable to be PRINTed in successive columns across the screen (usually 14 spaces apart). This is useful because, as you will see later on, much more information can be displayed on a screen and the data can be presented in a much more readable way.

Now type LIST.

Change the commas (,) on lines 7 to 12 to semicolons (;). (If you can't remember how, look back to where we changed the ends of the lines into commas.)

When you have done that, type LIST again to prove the changes have worked.

Now type RUN. What has happened?

There are now only small gaps (or perhaps no gaps at all) between each PRINTed number. A semicolon tells the computer to PRINT a number close to the previous one. This allows even more data to be crowded on the screen; and crowded is the correct word to use.

So now we can:

PRINT one number on each line;

PRINT in columns (by adding a comma after each item to be PRINTed);

PRINT one after another (by adding a semicolon after each item to be PRINTed).

We can also use a shorthand method of PRINTing. Try typing this exactly as shown:

```
7 PRINT A
8 PRINT B, C
9 PRINT D, E; F
10
11    (just type the line
12    numbers and press RETURN)
```

Type LIST and check that the changes have been correctly made, and that lines 1Ø, 11 and 12 have now disappeared. That's how we delete lines — we type in just the line numbers and press RETURN and the computer then erases those lines from its program listing.

Before you type RUN see if you can guess how the variables will PRINT.

Were you correct? If you were, well done! If you were wrong and know why you were wrong, well done! If you still don't know why, re-read this chapter before going any further — it will soon become clear to you.

Now see if you can change the program to PRINT three variables in columns and the other three variables next to each other on the next line.

5

The INPUT statement and loops

In this chapter, we shall introduce two new words to use in your programs — INPUT and GOTO.

When the computer sees the word INPUT in a statement, it will wait for you to enter something at the keyboard. The computer will then carry on through the program executing the statements in order as usual and using what you have entered. Let's try a program which could help you to learn your tables if you don't already know them!

First, type NEW to clear your computer's memory, then type in this program:

```
1 INPUT A
2 LET B = 3*A
3 PRINT B
4 END
```

If you now RUN the program the computer will read line 1 and know from the statement, INPUT A, that it must ask you to enter a

number. The usual way it does this is to display a question mark (?) or the letter L on the screen. If you now type in a number (it can be any number but for the moment, just type a number between 1 and 12), and press RETURN, the computer will give Box A in its memory the value of that number. So, if you type in 5, the variable A will be given a value of 5.

Then the computer will read line 2 and LET B have the value of 3 × A. If you typed in a 5, the value of B will now be 15. In response to line 3, the computer now displays (or PRINTs) the value of B on the screen.

Now type RUN again, and when the ? or L is displayed, type in a different number. Try lots of different numbers and see if it works every time.

If you didn't know your 3 times table, you could use this program to learn it. If you wanted to know the answer to 9 times 3, you would type 9 when the ? was displayed and the computer would give you the answer.

Now for the GOTO statement. As you know, the computer usually executes program statements in line number order. It first looks for a line number 1 and if there is one it executes it. If there isn't one it looks for a line number 2, then 3, and so on until it finds one. It then executes that statement in that line and goes on to the next number in order. You can change that order by including in your program a statement which tells the computer to GOTO a particular line number. For instance, you could change line 4 of your last program to read:

4 GOTO 1

(Remember that to change a line you just type the line again with the new statement.)

You can then RUN the program again in the same way as before and it will do all the things it did before in exactly the same way. However, when the computer gets to line 4, instead of just stopping it will now GOTO line 1. It will then execute line 1 and ask you for a number as it did before. So, if you wanted to practise your 3 times table you would just keep INPUTing different numbers each time the computer asked you to do so and it would give you the answers.

If you wanted to learn your 7 times table you would change line 2 to read:

    2 LET B = 7 * A

then any number you typed in would be multiplied by 7 by the computer and the answer PRINTed on the screen.

The program is now in a 'loop'. This means that it gets to line number 4 then it is told to go back to the beginning (line 1) and start all over again, so it never actually gets to the end of the program! It will keep on RUNning the program over and over again until you 'break' the loop; usually by pressing the CONTROL and C keys at the same time, or perhaps the STOP or the BREAK key. Your computer's instruction book will help you if none of these works. If you are really desperate you can, of course, switch off your computer but you will lose your program.

You have now learnt to use the GOTO statement. You will find this statement extremely useful when you get on to more complicated programs as it can also do other clever things for you — we shall learn about them in a later chapter.

6

More PRINTing and editing

Type this program into your machine. Remember to type NEW first to clear your computer's memory. Don't worry about the strange characters for the moment, we shall explain them later on. BUT do copy each character faithfully and put your own words in line 4.

```
1 PRINT "WHAT DO YOU THINK"
2 PRINT "OF THE SHOW SO FAR?"
3 PRINT
4 PRINT "(Put your own words in here)"
```

Now RUN.

Let's take each line in turn.

Line 1 PRINT "WHAT DO YOU THINK".

The quotation marks (") are the important feature. What is happening is that the computer is being told to PRINT the words

WHAT DO YOU THINK OF THE SHOW SO FAR?

17

WHAT DO YOU THINK. It PRINTs no more and no less than the words in between the quotation marks.

Line 2 is much the same!

Line 3 is an instruction to PRINT a line of blanks! Strange? Not really, because this has left a convenient space between the first two lines and whatever you typed in line 4. A statement containing just the keyword PRINT will cause the computer to PRINT a line of blanks before it PRINTs the next line.

If you change line 1 to read:

   1 PRINT WHAT DO YOU THINK

leaving out the quotation marks, the statement will not work, proving the need to use quotation marks for words to be PRINTed.

Now try writing your own program using PRINT and then any words you like. Remember that you must put quotation marks ('') both before and after the words you want PRINTed.

The computer can also 'remember' words in its memory boxes in exactly the same way as it did with numbers. There is just one small difference; to get the computer to remember words you must use a $ sign after the memory box name — A$, B$, C$, etc. These memory boxes, which are called 'ALPHABETIC' or 'STRING' VARIABLES, can also be used to remember numbers but, unlike numeric variables, the computer will not allow you to do sums with them.

Try this. Type:

   1 LET A$ = ''I''
   2 LET B$ = '' LOVE''
   3 LET C$ = '' SCHOOL''
   4 PRINT A$; B$; C$

(Be careful to leave spaces before the words LOVE and SCHOOL.)

Now RUN this very short program and you will see that the contents of the three memory boxes have been PRINTed one after the other because of the semicolons in line 4. (You may feel you would like to try this particular program again using a different word in line 2!)

Do not get confused between PRINTing words between quotation marks ('') and actually placing words in memory boxes. In the first program in this chapter you were just instructing the computer to PRINT words on the screen. In the second program you were telling the computer to put words into its memory boxes A$, B$ and C$, and then PRINT the contents of those boxes.

You have now used one of the most powerful tools of your computer. That is the ability to remember lots of words. It may not seem powerful at the moment but later on you will see what we mean.

7

A program to try

You have now learnt how to program a computer! You know about line numbers, how to give the computer instructions and how the computer can remember both numbers and letters and do various clever things with them. Now use this new-found knowledge to get the computer to work out for you how many drinks you have drunk in your life!

You will first get the computer to ask you how many drinks you have each day, then how old you are. It will then multiply the number of years you have lived by the number of days in a year, then it will multiply the answer by the number of drinks you have each day to find the total number you have drunk in your lifetime.

So here is the program. First type NEW and press RETURN to make sure there is nothing in your computer's memory. Now type in your program as follows exactly as it is written:

```
 5 LET C = Ø
1Ø PRINT "HOW OLD ARE YOU?"
2Ø INPUT A
3Ø PRINT "HOW MANY DRINKS DO"
4Ø PRINT "YOU HAVE EACH DAY?"
5Ø INPUT B
6Ø LET C = A * 365 * B
7Ø PRINT "YOU HAVE DRUNK ABOUT"
8Ø PRINT C
9Ø PRINT "DRINKS IN YOUR LIFE"
1ØØ END
```

You will have noticed that this time we have numbered our lines, 1Ø, 2Ø, 3Ø, and so on instead of 1, 2, 3 as before. This is the usual way of numbering lines and is done so that you can put extra lines in between the existing ones if you wish to later.

The program is quite easy to understand.

In line 1∅, the computer PRINTs the first question on the screen.

Line 2∅ tells the computer that it must wait for you to INPUT a number and to give its memory Box 'A' the value of that number.

Lines 3∅ and 4∅ ask the next question and line 5∅ waits for the answer from you.

Line 6∅ actually works out the answer by multiplying your age (A) by the number of days in a year (365) and then multiplying that figure by the number of drinks you have each day (B).

Lines 7∅ and 9∅ tell the computer to PRINT the answer to your problem with the actual number of drinks (C in line 8∅) in between.

So there you have a complete computer program which uses numbers and letters to ask you questions and to give you the answers so you can easily understand them.

The answer the computer gives you in this program will not be quite exact for two reasons. Firstly, you can only guess at how many drinks you have each day. Let's suppose you have a drink first thing in the morning, then another at breakfast and one during the morning at school and one at lunch. That's 4 so far — you must decide about how many you have during the whole day. It will be what is called an approximate number; that is a number which is about right and which will give a good idea of how many drinks you have on average. The second reason for the answer not being exact is that, in this program, you must put your age to the nearest year — do not bother about the extra months.

Now RUN the program if you haven't already done so and see if it acts like we said it would. If it doesn't, type LIST and check carefully that you have typed the program in correctly.

We can make this program even better. Don't switch the computer off or type NEW; type these extra lines:

```
5 PRINT "WHAT IS YOUR NAME?"
6 INPUT N$
65 PRINT "WELL"
66 PRINT N$
```

If you now type LIST and press RETURN you will see the whole program with the extra lines 5, 6, 65 and 66 in their correct places. If you now RUN this program, not only will the computer ask you how many drinks and how old you are, it will also ask you your name in line 5 and wait for your answer in line 6. (You will have noticed that we had to use a $ memory box to hold your name, just as we did to remember words to be PRINTed.) Then, at the end, the computer will use the N$ memory box to tell *you* the answer and mention your name again. Even better!

Now type in these extra lines:

```
95 PRINT
96 PRINT
97 PRINT "NEXT PERSON"
1ØØ GOTO 5
```

You can now try the program on several different people without having to type RUN each time.

8

SAVE and LOAD statements

By now you will probably be wishing that you didn't always lose your program every time you turned off your computer. It sometimes takes a long time to type in a program, and with one flick of the switch it is all lost. With some programs this doesn't matter, but some you might want to RUN again and it would be nice to be able to store them for later use. You may already know that there is a way to SAVE your programs and this is what we shall talk about now.

Most computers have some method of SAVEing programs. If your computer was very expensive it might have a diskette drive, but the most common way of SAVEing is to use an ordinary cassette recorder/player. Once connected to your computer, it is not much more difficult to record a computer program than it is to record a radio programme.

The problem is that, while it is not difficult to SAVE your programs on a cassette, each computer uses a slightly different method to do it.

Because of this we would suggest that you get someone to read your computer's instruction manual with you and practise SAVEing a two or three-line program (which *you* should write). Once SAVEd, the manual will explain how to LOAD the program back into your computer. It is worth spending some time practising both the SAVEing and LOADing of programs as nothing will be more annoying than finding that you have lost a precious program because of some simple recording error. Always spend time checking each action before going on to the next stage.

If you can get help then perhaps you will not need to read the rest of this chapter, but for those of you who have to work out how to SAVE programs by yourselves, we shall try to explain the most usual way of SAVEing programs in the hope that it will be of some use to you. Firstly, let us explain what we are trying to do.

When we have typed our program into the computer, we will lose

WHY SHOULD HE BE ABLE TO REMEMBER THINGS WHEN HE'S SWITCHED OFF—I CAN'T

that program if we turn off the power supply. If we want to keep that program we must record it. Most computer manufacturers supply information on how to connect a cassette recorder to the computer (if it isn't already a part of the computer) and often supply the necessary wires to make this connection. Usually one wire from the computer will go to the microphone socket on the cassette recorder, and a second to the earpiece socket. If you do get them the wrong way round you will not damage your cassette or computer, but you won't be able to record your program! Only your computer manual will tell you exactly which wire goes where.

Once connected, and you have your program ready for SAVEing, you press the record keys on your cassette recorder, then type SAVE on your computer and press RETURN. The computer will now send the program to the recorder for the program to be SAVEd on tape. When the recording is finished the screen will come back to you with O.K. or READY or something similar. Check your manual for your own computer.

To get the SAVEd program back into your computer's memory you will need to rewind your tape to the place just before you started recording. Type NEW to clear out any existing program you may have in memory and then type LOAD. Press the play key on your recorder and your program should be LOADed back into your computer. Once again the screen will let you know when LOADing has finished. You can prove this by typing LIST and seeing if your program is there. You may find that the volume and/or tone control adjustments are critical so keep trying until you get them just right and remember the settings for future use.

We are the first to agree that this sounds rather complicated, but we can assure you that if you read your manual and follow what it says, slowly and carefully, you will soon find there is nothing to worry about.

Time spent practising the SAVEing and LOADing of your programs will be well spent, so we do suggest that you pay particular attention to getting it right at this stage.

23

9

IF THEN statements for numbers

In this chapter, we shall look at a new statement called IF THEN.

Up to now, we have given the computer various statements such as PRINT, GOTO, LET. When we use IF THEN, we can still give the computer these statements but the computer will only perform them if a certain fact is true.

To see what we mean, type in this program (type NEW first):

```
1Ø INPUT A
2Ø IF A = 5 THEN GOTO 5Ø
3Ø PRINT "TRY AGAIN"
4Ø GOTO 1Ø
5Ø PRINT "GOT IT"
6Ø END
```

You will see the IF THEN statement in line 2Ø.

Now RUN the program and when the computer asks you to INPUT a number, INPUT a 5. When you press RETURN, the computer will give its memory box A the value of 5, then it will read the next highest line number as usual which in this program is line 2Ø. This line says IF A = 5 THEN GOTO 5Ø. The computer will ask itself the question 'Does A = 5?' Because the answer is 'yes', the computer will obey the final part of that line which is THEN GOTO 5Ø. When it gets to line 5Ø it will PRINT 'GOT IT', then it will go to line 6Ø and END.

Now try RUNning the program again but this time, when the computer asks you to INPUT a number, INPUT a 7. What happens? The computer should PRINT 'TRY AGAIN' on the screen and wait for you to INPUT another number. Do you understand why? When the computer reads line 2Ø it asks itself the question again, 'Does A = 5?' This time of course it doesn't, because you told the computer to give A the value of 7. So the computer takes no notice of the rest of the line, it just goes on to the next line (line 3∅), which tells it to PRINT 'TRY AGAIN'. Then, line 4∅ tells it to GOTO 1∅ and wait for the INPUT of another number.

The 'IF A = 5' part of the statement is called a 'Condition'. We can talk about a condition being true or untrue. In our program, if A does equal 5, the condition will be true. If A is equal to anything other than 5, the condition will be untrue.

So, to remind you, if the condition in an IF THEN statement is true, the computer will do whatever you tell it to in the rest of that line. If it is not true, the computer will take no notice of the remaining instructions in that line and will simply go to the next line.

IF THE LIGHT IS GREEN THEN CROSS THE ROAD

Some lines from computer programs are shown on the next page. They are not complete programs, just parts of programs so don't attempt to RUN them. Imagine you are the computer reading these programs. When you read an IF THEN statement you must decide which statement line you (the computer) will read next. Read through the programs and write the number of the next line you will GOTO in the box.

In line 13∅ of the first example for instance, if the condition A = B were true, the computer would obey the instruction and GOTO 18∅. However, in this case the condition is not true (because A = 5 and B = 7), so the computer would take no notice of the remaining instructions in line 13∅ and would just go on to the next line, which is 14∅. The number to write in the box is therefore 14∅. Now do the rest of the examples. If you have any problems, the answers are on page 29.

Example 1
```
11Ø LET A = 5
12Ø LET B = 7
13Ø IF A = B THEN GOTO 18Ø
14Ø GOTO 2ØØØ
```

Example 2
```
6Ø LET A = 5
7Ø LET B = 5
8Ø IF A = B THEN GOTO 1Ø
9Ø GOTO 13Ø
```

Example 3
```
1ØØØ LET A = 7
1Ø1Ø LET B = 5
1Ø2Ø IF A = B THEN GOTO 2ØØØ
1Ø3Ø GOTO 12Ø
```

Example 4
```
12 LET B = 7
23 LET A = 5
34 IF A = B THEN GOTO 1ØØ
45 GOTO 14Ø
```

Example 5
```
12Ø LET A = 599
13Ø LET B = 599
14Ø IF B = A THEN GOTO 6Ø
15Ø GOTO 83Ø
```

What we have done in our examples is to make comparisons between A and B to see if they are equal. To do this we have used the equals sign (=).

At school, you have probably met these other signs:

< means 'LESS THAN'
> means 'GREATER THAN'

To say that 7 is less than 9, we can write:
7 < 9.

5 is greater than 4 can be written as:

5 > 4.

When we make comparisons in an IF THEN statement, we can use the < and > signs as well as the = sign.

Here is a program to try. As this is a new program, type NEW to clear out the previous program from the computer's memory.

```
1∅ PRINT "ENTER A NUMBER UP TO 1∅"
2∅ INPUT N
3∅ IF N < 5 THEN GOTO 7∅
4∅ IF N > 5 THEN GOTO 1∅∅
5∅ PRINT "YOUR NUMBER IS FIVE"
6∅ END
7∅ PRINT "YOUR NUMBER IS LESS THAN FIVE"
8∅ PRINT "TRY AGAIN"
9∅ GOTO 2∅
1∅∅ PRINT "YOUR NUMBER IS GREATER THAN FIVE"
11∅ PRINT "TRY AGAIN"
12∅ GOTO 2∅
```

When you have typed in the program, RUN it and enter a number between 1 and 10. The computer will give memory box N the value of your number.

If your number is less than 5, the condition N < 5 in line 3∅ will be true, so the computer *will* obey the instruction in that line and GOTO 7∅.

If your number is greater than 5, the condition N < 5 in line 3∅ will not be true, so the computer will go on to read the next line, line 4∅. Here the condition *will* be true so the computer will GOTO 1∅∅.

If the number you INPUT is 5, then neither of the conditions in lines 3∅ or 4∅ will be true, so the computer will go on to line 5∅ and PRINT 'YOUR NUMBER IS FIVE'.

Try RUNning the program several times and make sure you understand what the computer is doing.

Here are three more comparison signs:—

<= means LESS THAN OR EQUAL TO
>= means GREATER THAN OR EQUAL TO
<> means NOT EQUAL TO

These comparison signs can all be used in IF THEN statements in exactly the same way as the = or < or > signs. We shall leave them for the moment, though.

To finish this chapter, we shall build up a program using our new knowledge. Don't forget to clear out the previous program by typing NEW, then enter the following program making sure you use the line numbers shown:

```
3Ø PRINT "ENTER A NUMBER BETWEEN 1 AND 1ØØ"
 4Ø INPUT N
1ØØ PRINT "TRY TO GUESS THE NUMBER"
11Ø INPUT G
125 REM OPTIONAL CLEAR SCREEN
13Ø IF G < N THEN GOTO 17Ø
14Ø IF G > N THEN GOTO 19Ø
15Ø PRINT "CORRECT"
16Ø GOTO 3Ø
17Ø PRINT "TOO LOW — TRY AGAIN"
18Ø GOTO 1ØØ
19Ø PRINT "TOO HIGH — TRY AGAIN"
2ØØ GOTO 1ØØ
```

Now RUN the program and enter a number. With your hand or a piece of paper, cover up the number on the screen and ask a friend to guess it. You will see that the computer uses IF THEN statements to help your friend guess the number.

It's a good program, but it is a pity you can see the secret number, so let us add some empty PRINT lines to force it off the screen. With certain computers you will not need this routine as the secret number will not remain on the screen. Have a look at the routine though, and understand how it works.

```
1Ø LET X = Ø
7Ø LET X = X + 1
8Ø PRINT
9Ø IF X < 4Ø THEN GOTO 7Ø
```

Line 7Ø adds 1 to the value of memory box X and then puts the new value back into X. Line 8Ø PRINTs a blank line. While the value of X is still less than 40, the condition in line 9Ø is true and the computer loops back to line 7Ø, adds 1 to X and PRINTs another blank line. When, eventually, X is worth 40, the condition in line 9Ø is no longer true and the computer goes on to the next highest line number which is 1ØØ.

Now alter line 16Ø to read:

```
16Ø GOTO 1Ø
```

to ensure that the program restarts from the correct line. RUN the program and watch the improvement.

Most computers will continue to PRINT lines of information on to the screen, even if all the screen is filled up. They do this by moving all the lines up one so that there is a blank line available at the bottom of the screen. This is called 'autoscrolling'.

If your computer stops RUNning a program because the screen is full, you will need to add to that program a line containing a clear screen statement (usually 'CLS' or 'HOME'). The best place for such a statement is usually immediately following an INPUT statement. In the above program we have added a REM statement at line 125 to show you the best place, and we shall continue to do this in future programs to assist you.

REM is short for REMark. REM statements are used to make comments, or to label programs. When the computer reads a REM statement it knows that it must take no notice of the rest of that line. You may write whatever you like after the REM because the computer will ignore it. We shall use REM statements occasionally in later programs to give you reminders or help.

Now let us control what is INPUT at line 4∅. Add:

```
5∅ IF N <    1 THEN GOTO 3∅
6∅ IF N >1∅∅ THEN GOTO 3∅
```

Now, the computer will not allow you to enter a number which is less than 1 (zero or a minus number) or more than 100.

And now for a touch of class! Add:

```
2∅ LET T = ∅
12∅ LET T = T + 1
15∅ PRINT "CORRECT IN "; T; " TRIES"
```

'A TOUCH OF CLASS'

Now we are using a counting routine to count how many guesses are made, by adding 1 to memory box T for each guess. The contents are then printed out in line 15∅.

This is a good program which should give you plenty of fun.

Answers to the questions on page 26.

Example 1	14∅	4	45
2	1∅	5	6∅
3	1∅3∅		

10

IF . . . THEN statements for words

In the last chapter you learnt about the IF THEN statement and used it in some programs. You gave the computer 'conditions' and told it to do things only if those conditions were true.

By using the word 'OR', we can give the computer two conditions in one IF THEN statement and tell it to do something if at least one of the conditions is true. Here is a program using an 'OR' statement (in line 4∅):

```
1∅ PRINT "ENTER A NUMBER"
2∅ PRINT "BETWEEN 5 AND 1∅"
3∅ INPUT N
4∅ IF N < 5 OR N > 1∅ THEN GOTO 1∅
5∅ PRINT "THANK YOU"
6∅ END
```

Type in this program (remembering to type NEW first), and RUN it. You will see that line 4∅ says that if N is less than 5 OR N is greater than 10, the computer must GOTO line 1∅. This means that the computer will only say "THANK YOU" if you INPUT a number between 5 and 10. You will see that by using the word OR, we can now control what is INPUT with a one-line statement. This saves typing time and makes your listing more readable and understandable.

Another keyword that can be used in an IF THEN statement is 'AND'. When you use 'AND', both the conditions must be true if the computer is to obey the instruction at the end of the line. Type NEW and enter this:

```
1∅ PRINT "INPUT A NUMBER"
2∅ INPUT A
3∅ PRINT "INPUT ANOTHER NUMBER"
4∅ INPUT B
5∅ IF A = 5 AND B = 6 THEN GOTO 7∅
```

```
6Ø GOTO 1Ø
7Ø PRINT "THANK YOU"
8Ø END
```

You can see that only if A = 5 AND B = 6 will the computer obey the instruction and GOTO 7Ø. If, for instance, you were to INPUT the number 5 into A and 7 into B, the first condition (A = 5) would be true, but the second condition (B = 6) would not be true. The computer would just go on to read line 6Ø which tells it to GOTO 1Ø. Only if the numbers you enter are 5 and 6 will the computer GOTO 7Ø and PRINT "THANK YOU".

The IF THEN statement can be used to make comparisons between words as well as numbers. Type NEW and then enter this program:

```
1Ø PRINT "ENTER YOUR PASSWORD"
2Ø INPUT P$
3Ø IF P$<>"BATMAN" THEN GOTO 1Ø
5Ø PRINT "YOUR PASSWORD IS CORRECT"
6Ø END
```

This program works in exactly the same way as our other programs using IF THEN statements, but instead of asking you to INPUT a number, the computer asks you to INPUT letters. Line 3∅ says that if P$ does not equal "BATMAN" THEN GOTO 1∅ and PRINT "ENTER YOUR PASSWORD". You will see that the computer will only allow you to go on if you enter the correct password.

This sort of password control is used a lot in large computers which only certain people are allowed to use. The Police computer for instance, has a tremendous amount of information in it which only a few people may see. The computer only allows those who know the password to use it, and they must keep their password secret.

Now for a program which uses OR and AND in IF THEN statements to compare both numbers and letters. This program will tell you whether or not you are allowed to see a particular film at a cinema. You probably know the rules for going to see films:

To see an X film you must be 18 or over.
To see an AA film you must be 14 or over.
A and U films may be seen by anyone.

Type NEW and enter this program:

```
1∅ REM   THIS PROGRAM TELLS YOU
2∅ REM   IF YOU MAY GO
3∅ REM   TO SEE A FILM
4∅ PRINT "IS THE FILM AN X, AA, A OR U?"
5∅ INPUT F$
6∅ IF F$ = "X" OR F$ = "AA" OR F$ = "A" OR
   F$ = "U" THEN GOTO 8∅
7∅ GOTO 4∅
8∅ PRINT "WHAT IS YOUR AGE"
9∅ INPUT A
```

```
100 IF F$ = "X" AND A> = 18 THEN GOTO 150
110 IF F$ = "AA" AND A> = 14 THEN GOTO 150
120 IF F$ = "A" OR F$ = "U" THEN GOTO 150
130 PRINT "YOU MAY NOT GO"
140 END
150 PRINT "GO AND ENJOY THE FILM"
160 END
```

Let us go through the program line by line to make sure you understand how it works:

Lines 10, 20 and 30: these are REM statements.

Line 40: asks you what sort of film you want to see.

Line 50: tells the computer to store what you INPUT in its memory box F$.

Line 60: checks that what you INPUT into F$ is X or AA or A or U. If you did not INPUT any of these then your INPUT was incorrect and

Line 70: tells the computer to go back to line 40 and ask you for INPUT again.

Line 80: asks you for your age.

Line 90: accepts your age and puts it into memory box A.

Line 100: if the film is an X and you are 18 or over, the computer is told to GOTO 150 where it PRINTS "GO AND ENJOY THE FILM".

Line 110: if the film is an AA and you are 14 or over, the computer is again told to GOTO 150.

Line 120: if the film is an A or U, anyone may go and see it so, once again, the computer goes to line 150.

Line 130: if none of the above conditions has been true, then you may not go to see the film and the computer will tell you so.

Type in the program (don't forget NEW) and RUN it. Give various answers to the questions and check that the program RUNs as it should. The program looks a little confusing at first but we do suggest that you follow it through and make sure you understand how it works.

If the computer says you may go, we hope that you will enjoy the film!

11

FOR . . . NEXT loops

Cast your mind back to Chapter 9 — to the program we wrote which asked you to guess a number. Do you remember the little routine we added to that program which PRINTed 4Ø blank lines so that the secret number did not stay on the screen? Here is that routine again:

```
1Ø LET X = Ø
7Ø LET X = X + 1
8Ø PRINT
9Ø IF X < 4Ø THEN GOTO 7Ø
```

It is called a 'routine' because, although it would work as a program by itself, we actually used it as just part of our larger program.

You will remember that the routine kept looping back to line 7Ø, adding 1 to the value of X each time before PRINTing a blank line. It kept doing this until X was worth 40.

THERE GOES THAT SECRET NUMBER — BUT I STILL KNOW WHAT IT IS!

Now type the routine into your computer again, as above, but with just one small change. Type line 8∅ like this:

8∅ PRINT X,

What do you think will happen when you RUN it? Try it and see. The computer should PRINT all the numbers from 1 to 40. Each time the computer gets to line 8∅ it PRINTs X, and as X is being increased by 1 each time the routine loops round, you get a long list of numbers.

There is an easier way of doing this using a statement called FOR . . . NEXT . . . STEP. To show you how it works, we shall use it to do the same as we did above and PRINT 40 numbers again. Type NEW, then enter this routine:

6∅ FOR X = 1 TO 4∅ STEP 1
7∅ PRINT X,
8∅ NEXT X
9∅ END

When you RUN it, the computer should PRINT out all the numbers from 1 to 40 in just the same way as it did with our earlier routine. This is how it works:

Line 6∅ tells the computer that memory box X is to be given values from 1 to 40 in STEPs of 1. This means that the first time the computer reads line 6∅ it will give X a value of 1. It will then continue down through the lines of the routine, performing each line as usual until it reaches the NEXT statement. At this point it adds the STEP (of 1, in our routine) to X and loops round again, so the second time the computer reads line 6∅, X will have the value of 2, then the third time the value of 3, then 4, then 5 and so on until X is worth 40 when the routine will END.

See if you can guess what will happen if you were to change the number following STEP to a 2 and then to a 5. Try it to see if you were right.

If you want to, you can change line 7∅ so that instead of PRINTing the value of X, it PRINTs your own name 40 times:

7∅ PRINT " "

Type your name inside the " " marks.

We are sorry to mention tables again, but here is a program which will PRINT out the table of your choice with no trouble at all! Type NEW.

1∅ REM TABLES PROGRAM
2∅ PRINT "ENTER THE TIMES"
3∅ PRINT "TABLE YOU WANT"
4∅ INPUT T

```
5Ø FOR X = 1 TO 12 STEP 1
6Ø LET Z = X * T
7Ø PRINT X; " TIMES "; T; " = "; Z
8Ø NEXT X
9Ø END
```

Type the program into your computer. (Did someone say something about typing NEW first? We shall not be mentioning it again. Just try to remember to type NEW before typing in any new programs.)

When the computer asks you for a number, enter a number between 1 and 12. The computer should then PRINT the table from 1 through to 12 times.

You will see the FOR statement in line 5Ø and the NEXT statement in line 8Ø. X is being given values from 1 to 12. In line 6Ø we are telling the computer to give Z the value of X times T and then PRINTing the answer in line 7Ø. The program keeps looping round lines 5Ø and 8Ø until X is equal to 12, when the program ENDs.

Here is another use for FOR . . . NEXT . . . STEP statements. Enter this NEW program:

```
4Ø FOR D = 1 TO 1ØØ STEP 1
45 NEXT D
5Ø PRINT "THANK YOU"
7Ø END
```

RUN the program. Did you notice a delay before the computer PRINTed "THANK YOU"? Now change line 4Ø to:

```
4Ø FOR D = 1 TO 1ØØØ STEP 1
```

Now RUN the program again. There should have been a longer delay this time. Can you see what is happening? The computer is looping between lines 45 and 40. This takes some time to perform, so it makes a delay! You can see that we can alter the delay by changing the number that D is set to. Now type these extra lines:

```
2Ø PRINT "ENTER A NUMBER UP TO 999999"
3Ø INPUT T
4Ø FOR D = 1 TO T STEP 1
```

This will let you change the delay — the higher the number, the longer the delay. RUN the program a few times and INPUT various numbers.

Now for some fun! Go and get a watch with a second hand on it or a digital watch that shows seconds. We are going to see how many loops your computer will do in 1 minute. INPUT T so that it is 999999 and press your RETURN key. Time *exactly* 1 minute and then press your BREAK key or CONTROL and C keys as we did at the end of Chapter 5 to stop the program looping. We now need to find out what value D has reached, so type PRINT D (in immediate mode — remember Chapter 2). This number might be anything from 3000 to 999999. Write it down on a piece of paper because we shall need it in later programs.

Now you can have contests with your friends to see who can get the computer to stop closest to a chosen number. Decide on a number, say 3456, INPUT 999999 into T again and press RETURN, then take it in turns to RUN and stop the computer when you think the value has reached the number you decided upon. The person who is closest is the winner!

The following program will let you use your computer as a timer. You will see that line 7Ø has nnnn in it. When typing in the program, don't type in the nnnn, but in its place type in the number you wrote down earlier.

```
1Ø REM TIMER
2Ø PRINT
3Ø PRINT "INPUT G TO GET GOING"
4Ø INPUT G$
5Ø FOR D = 1 TO 999999 STEP 1
6Ø NEXT D
7Ø LET S = D/ nnnn * 6Ø
8Ø PRINT
9Ø PRINT "YOU TOOK  "; S; "  SECONDS"
1ØØ GOTO 2Ø
```

Now RUN and INPUT the letter G. As soon as you press RETURN the program will start looping between lines 5Ø and 6Ø. To stop it press BREAK or CONTROL and C as before, then type GOTO 7∅. (We type GOTO 7∅ because that is where we want the computer to pick up the program, and with our looping/timing number left in memory box D. If we were to RUN it would start at line 1∅ again and wipe out the number stored in D.)

The computer will display the number of seconds between you pressing G and stopping the program. Line 7∅ is the line that works out the number of seconds; it divides D by the number of loops completed in one minute, then multiplies the answer by 60 to get the time in seconds.

12

RND and INT statements

We shall now meet two new keywords called INT and RND. They will often appear together in program lines but they can also be used separately. We shall deal with them separately to start with and afterwards see how they may be used together.

INT is short for INTeger and means a whole number. Whole numbers are numbers like 5 or 6 or 234. They haven't got any figures after decimal points. The numbers 5·6 or 14·75 or 354·5 have got figures after decimal points so they are not INTegers.

In Chapter 1 we said that some computers only work in whole numbers and then suggested that you divide 9 by 5 to see if your computer is one of these. If the answer was shown as 1 it means that your computer uses the programming language called INTEGER BASIC, and it will always give its answers in whole numbers. If the answer was shown as 1·8 your computer uses the FLOATING-POINT BASIC language and can work with numbers which have figures after a decimal point. You can use INT to make FLOATING-POINT BASIC look like INTEGER BASIC, but it is not possible to make INTEGER BASIC into FLOATING-POINT BASIC. This doesn't mean that INTEGER BASIC is not such a good language, it is just different.

If your computer uses FLOATING-POINT BASIC, you should now read the following section. If not, we suggest you skip through it quickly and then go straight on to the section about RND.

Let us see how INTeger works. Type in this very short program:

```
1Ø LET A = 4·7
2Ø PRINT A
3Ø PRINT INT(A)
4Ø END
```

When RUN, the computer will first give memory box A the value

39

of 4·7 and will then PRINT A (which will be 4·7). Then it will PRINT just the INTeger part of A which is the whole number, leaving off the decimal parts. The INTeger of A is therefore 4; any figures that are not whole numbers are just left off.

This is the usual way in which computers deal with INTegers. However, some computers work in a slightly different way from this. To help you understand exactly how your own computer changes numbers with decimal parts into INTegers, type in the following program:

```
1Ø PRINT "ENTER A NUMBER WITH"
2Ø PRINT "A DECIMAL POINT IN IT"
3Ø INPUT N
4Ø PRINT "GUESS THE INTEGER"
45 PRINT
5Ø INPUT I
55 REM OPTIONAL CLEAR SCREEN
6Ø IF I = INT(N) THEN GOTO 1ØØ
7Ø PRINT "NO THE ANSWER IS  "; INT(N)
75 PRINT
8Ø PRINT "TRY ANOTHER"
9Ø GOTO 1Ø
1ØØ PRINT "CORRECT — TRY ANOTHER"
11Ø GOTO 1Ø
```

Now try INPUTing all sorts of numbers, some with decimal parts and some without. Try to guess what the INTegers of those numbers will be. As we said before, the computer will probably just leave off the decimal parts, but that may not be the case if you INPUT a minus number! INPUT −9·9 and then guess −9 for the INTeger. If that is not right you will find that −10 will work. This looks odd, but if you think about it, −10 is a lower number than −9·9 (just like 4 is a lower number than 4·7). Continue trying numbers, both ordinary numbers e.g. 33·4, 13·9, and also minus numbers e.g. −34·6, −56·3, −1·1, until you guess each one correctly. This will mean that you fully understand how your computer works out its INTegers.

There are many times when answers to sums will have decimal parts which aren't needed in programs. It is in these instances that we shall use INT so that we can use just the whole number part. We shall come back to INT later, but for the moment let us look at RND.

The letters RND are short for RaNDom. The word 'random' means haphazard or any-old-how. If we ask the computer to choose a RaNDom number it is rather like picking a number out of a hat or throwing a dice — we don't know what number it will be. RND is often used in programs, such as games, programs, where we want the computer to supply numbers of its own. RND is like INT in that, with different computers, it can work in slightly different ways. For instance, some computers give RaNDom numbers that are always less than 1 such as ·000001 or ·444532 or ·765993 or ·999999. Other computers give whole numbers (INTegers) such as 312 or 5 or 8412. This second type may look more useful but, with a little bit of clever programming, the first method can be just as good.

At this point you must look up RND in the BASIC manual that came with your own computer. That manual will tell you exactly how statements using RND should be typed. As we said earlier, the exact way differs from computer to computer.

Your RND statements may look like one of these:

RND
RND(X)
RND(∅)
RND(1)
RND(nnnn) — (The nnnn may be any number that you want it to be.)

GOOD, I CAN CHOOSE A NUMBER

In this book, our RND statements will always look like this:

RND(X)

If the manual with your computer says you must type RND statements in a slightly different form, then type in what your own computer needs.

Here are some possible RND statements with the type of numbers they might give. Is yours like one of these?

RND — might give a number up to, but not quite, 1.
RND(5) — might give a number between 1 and 5.
RND(1) — might give a number up to, but not quite, 1.

It will be up to you to find out which form your own computer takes.

From now on we shall assume that your computer uses FLOATING-POINT BASIC and we shall use INT to change numbers with decimal parts into whole numbers whenever that is necessary. Also, we shall often describe in a REM line what range of RaNDom numbers the computer is to supply. We shall do this so that, by referring to your own computer's manual, you will always be able to use the correct form of RaNDom statement in your program.

To finish this chapter, we shall use both INT and RND to make the computer throw some dice for us! Here is the program for you to type in and RUN:

```
 1Ø REM DICE
1ØØ PRINT "DO YOU WANT ONE OR"
2ØØ PRINT "TWO DICE TO THROW"
3ØØ INPUT N
4ØØ IF N = 1 OR N = 2 THEN GOTO 6ØØ
5ØØ GOTO 1ØØ
6ØØ PRINT "PRESS T TO THROW"
7ØØ INPUT T$
8ØØ PRINT
9ØØ PRINT
95Ø REM OPTIONAL CLEAR SCREEN
1ØØØ FOR R = 1 TO N STEP 1
11ØØ REM RANDOM NUMBER FROM 1 TO 6
12ØØ LET D = INT (RND(X) * 6) + 1
13ØØ PRINT D,
14ØØ NEXT R
15ØØ PRINT
16ØØ PRINT
17ØØ GOTO 6ØØ
```

You should by now be able to understand most of this program without any trouble and will see our two new keywords in line 12∅∅.

Line 12∅∅ is where the RaNDom number is thought up by the computer. To make it easier to explain we shall build up this line in stages. First, the computer is told to give memory box D a RaNDom number of anything up to, but not quite, 1:

LET D = RND(X)

That number is then multiplied by 6:

LET D = RND(X) * 6

This statement by itself would give a random number somewhere between ·000006 and 5·999994, but we need a number from 1 to 6 (the numbers on a dice) so we add 1 to the answer:

LET D = (RND(X) * 6) + 1

This means that the value of memory box D will now be between 1·000006 and 6·999994, so now we knock off any decimal parts of the number by using INT, leaving us with the line looking like this:

LET D = INT (RND(X) * 6) + 1

This will produce a RaNDom number from 1 to 6; just right for a dice.

Line 4∅∅ controls what you INPUT into memory box N. Only IF N = 1 OR N = 2 will the computer GOTO line 6∅∅ and continue performing the program. If N is anything else, the condition will not be true and the computer will go on to line 5∅∅ where it will be told to go back and ask you again.

You will see a FOR NEXT STEP loop between lines 1∅∅∅ and 14∅∅. This makes the computer loop round 'N' times so if you INPUT a 1 into memory box N (in line 3∅∅) the computer will give one RaNDom number. If you INPUT a 2, it will give two RaNDom numbers.

13

More about random numbers

In Chapter 12 we explained how to use RND and you saw how it worked in the program that threw some dice. In this chapter, we shall tell you one or two more things we think you ought to know about RND to understand fully how your own computer works with this keyword.

If you ran the dice program several times, you may have found that the results seemed to repeat themselves. This can happen with some computers because their choice of RaNDom numbers is not always completely haphazard. What happens is that a computer has a list of several hundred different numbers it can choose from. When a program asks for, say, two RaNDom numbers, the computer supplies the first two numbers from this list. When you RUN the program a second time it is possible that the computer will go to the beginning of this list again and supply the same two numbers.

This may seem rather strange but, as you will see later on, it can sometimes be quite useful. However, that doesn't help us with the dice program; you may think it's an excellent way of cheating your friends when you know what numbers will come up, but we don't want to encourage dishonesty so we will tell you how to get over the problem!

Once again, you must look at your own computer's manual because of the differences in the way that some computers work. What you need to do is to get your computer to start at a different place in its list of numbers every time you ask it for a RaNDom number. You may have to change the RND 'argument' (the figures in brackets after the word RND) or perhaps you will have to type the word RANDOM or RANDOMISE or RANDOMIZE at the beginning of the program, on a line all to itself.

Here is a program you can use to check if your own computer needs one of these changes in order to give you completely RaNDom numbers each time:

```
1Ø REM RANDOM NUMBER CHECK
2Ø FOR R = 1 TO 2Ø STEP 1
3Ø REM RANDOM NUMBER FROM 1 TO 1ØØ
4Ø LET X = INT (RND(X) * 1ØØ) + 1
5Ø PRINT X,
6Ø NEXT R
7Ø END
```

Now RUN the program. The computer should give you a list of twenty RaNDom numbers. Make a note of all the numbers on a piece of paper, then switch the computer off. Switch on again after a few moments and type the program in again. RUN it and check the numbers against your written list.

Are they the same as before? If they are, you will need to make one of the changes we mentioned. The most likely change needed is to put one of the above new words near the beginning of the program like this:

15 RANDOM (or RANDOMISE or RANDOMIZE)

Now when you RUN the program, you should get different RaNDom numbers each time. (Don't forget, your computer may need a change to the argument rather than one of the new words.) If you had problems with the dice program, perhaps you would like to make the necessary change and RUN it again to check that it will then give you truly RaNDom numbers.

To finish this chapter we are going to ask you to turn back to Chapter 9. Do you remember the program where one person thought of a number and another person had to guess it with help from the computer? When you got to the end of Chapter 9 the completed program should have looked like this:

```
1Ø LET X = Ø
2Ø LET T = Ø
3Ø PRINT "ENTER A NUMBER BETWEEN 1 AND 1ØØ"
```

```
40 INPUT N
50 IF N < 1 THEN GOTO 30
60 IF N > 100 THEN GOTO 30
65 REM OPTIONALLY REPLACE LINES 70, 80, 90 WITH
   CLEAR SCREEN STATEMENT
70 LET X = X + 1
80 PRINT
90 IF X < 40 THEN GOTO 70
100 PRINT "TRY TO GUESS THE NUMBER"
110 INPUT G
120 LET T = T + 1
130 IF G < N THEN GOTO 170
140 IF G > N THEN GOTO 190
150 PRINT "CORRECT IN   "; T ;"   TRIES"
160 GOTO 10
170 PRINT "TOO LOW — TRY AGAIN"
180 GOTO 100
190 PRINT "TOO HIGH — TRY AGAIN"
200 GOTO 100
```

Now you can use your new-found knowledge of RND to get the *computer* to think of a number which *you* can then try to guess. Here are the lines you will need to type in:

```
30 REM RANDOM NUMBER FROM 1 TO 100
40 LET N = INT (RND(X) * 100) + 1
50 (Just press RETURN)
60 (Just press RETURN)
153 FOR D = 1 to 300
156 NEXT D
```

Also remember you may need to change the argument or add the RANDOM statement to make sure you get a proper RaNDom number.

14

Subroutines

When we were working on the number-guessing program in Chapter 9, you may remember that we talked about 'routines'. Then, we said that a routine is really a small program which will work all by itself, but which is actually used as just part of a larger program. The routine we used in Chapter 9 PRINTed 40 blank lines so that the number to be guessed was not shown on the screen.

Sometimes we may need to use the same routine several times in one program. One way to do this would be to type all the lines of the routine wherever it was needed. It would be much easier though, if we could just type the routine once and then tell the computer to go and use it whenever we wanted it to (such a routine would be called a subroutine). There are a pair of keywords in BASIC which let us do exactly that! They are called GOSUB and RETURN.

GOSUB is short for 'GO to a SUBroutine'. It is rather like GOTO in that it tells the computer to jump to a line number. However, GOSUB is special because when the computer reads a line with GOSUB in, it makes a note of that line number before it jumps to the new part of the program. The computer then continues performing the program lines of the subroutine until it reaches a line containing the word RETURN. It then jumps back (RETURNs) to the line following the line number it had previously noted.

This diagram of a pretend program will help you to understand how it works:

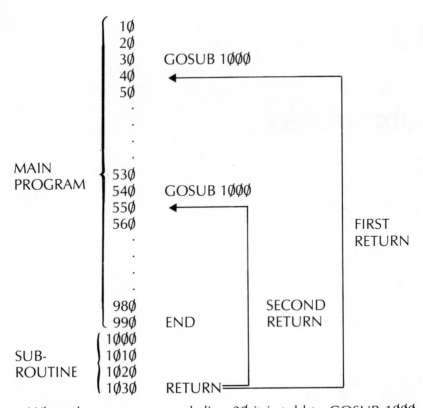

	1∅		
	2∅		
	3∅	GOSUB 1∅∅∅	
	4∅		
	5∅		
MAIN PROGRAM	53∅		
	54∅	GOSUB 1∅∅∅	
	55∅		
	56∅		FIRST RETURN
	98∅		SECOND RETURN
	99∅	END	
SUB-ROUTINE	1∅∅∅		
	1∅1∅		
	1∅2∅		
	1∅3∅	RETURN	

When the computer reads line 3∅ it is told to GOSUB 1∅∅∅. It makes a note of the line number in which the GOSUB appeared (line 3∅), because later on it will have to RETURN to the next line number. When it gets to line 1∅∅∅, it performs each line in order until it gets to line 1∅3∅. The computer has remembered where it was when it read the GOSUB statement and it RETURNS to the next line after it — line 4∅. It then continues through the main program and acts in just the same way when it gets to line 54∅. This is very useful because our routine may be 'called' by just saying GOSUB 1∅∅∅ and this can be done from any line in the program.

So, the order in which the computer would action *all* the lines in this program would be as follows:

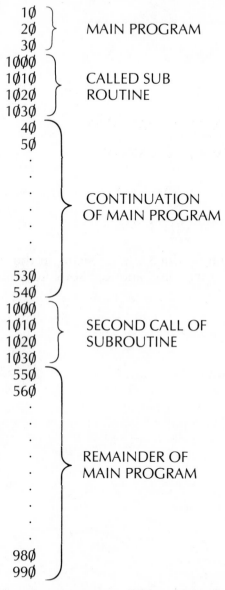

10 ⎫
20 ⎬ MAIN PROGRAM
30 ⎭

1000 ⎫
1010 ⎬ CALLED SUB
1020 ⎬ ROUTINE
1030 ⎭

40 ⎫
50 ⎪
. ⎪
. ⎪
. ⎬ CONTINUATION
. ⎪ OF MAIN PROGRAM
. ⎪
. ⎪
530 ⎪
540 ⎭

1000 ⎫
1010 ⎬ SECOND CALL OF
1020 ⎬ SUBROUTINE
1030 ⎭

550 ⎫
560 ⎪
. ⎪
. ⎪
. ⎬ REMAINDER OF
. ⎪ MAIN PROGRAM
. ⎪
. ⎪
. ⎪
980 ⎪
990 ⎭

Here is a program which, although it does not really make the best use of GOSUBs, will nevertheless show you just how they work. The program may look a little strange but don't be put off by its appearance. In lines 200 to 800 you will see a number of dots between Xs. Don't type the dots but just type spaces instead. The dots are there to show you how many spaces to type between the Xs.

```
1Ø REM GOSUB . . . RETURN
2Ø GOSUB 4ØØ
3Ø GOSUB 8ØØ
4Ø GOSUB 8ØØ
5Ø GOSUB 6ØØ
6Ø GOSUB 8ØØ
7Ø GOSUB 8ØØ
8Ø GOSUB 2ØØ
9Ø END
2ØØ PRINT "..X..X..XXXX..XXXX..XXXX..XXXX"
3ØØ RETURN
4ØØ PRINT "..X..X..XXXX..X.....X.....XXXX"
5ØØ RETURN
6ØØ PRINT "..XXXX..XXX...X.....X.....X..X"
7ØØ RETURN
8ØØ PRINT "..X..X..X.....X.....X.....X..X"
9ØØ RETURN
```

You will find some programs which use GOSUBs in the next chapter. Look in particular at the DICE and RUSSIAN ROULETTE programs.

15

Some simple programs

This chapter consists of four programs for you to try on your computer. The first two are fairly short and deal with numbers. The other two are longer and use PRINT statements to display pictures on the screen. These programs use most of the keywords that we have covered so far. A short description is given of each program.

Program 1. *** WHEEL OF FORTUNE ***
```
1Ø PRINT "*** WHEEL OF FORTUNE ***"
2Ø LET X = Ø
3Ø PRINT "WATCH THE NUMBERS SLOW DOWN"
4Ø PRINT "UNTIL IT STOPS AT THE WINNER"
5Ø LET X = INT (RND(X) * 1ØØ) + 1
6Ø FOR B = 1 TO 1Ø STEP 1
7Ø LET X = X + 2
8Ø PRINT B; "   ";
9Ø IF X > 2ØØ THEN GOTO 16Ø
1ØØ FOR D = 1 TO X + X STEP 1
11Ø NEXT D
12Ø NEXT B
13Ø PRINT
15Ø GOTO 6Ø
16Ø PRINT
17Ø PRINT
18Ø PRINT "THE WINNER IS NUMBER  "; B
19Ø END
```

This program could be useful at a school fete or fund-raising event. The numbers 1 to 10 PRINT out on your screen, each new number taking longer to PRINT, until the winning number is reached. The game is rather like roulette! Note that line 8Ø not only PRINTs out the value of B but also PRINTs a following space. If you

'WHEEL OF FORTUNE'

want to PRINT more, or fewer numbers, change the 'TO' number in line 6∅ to whatever you want it to be. If the game takes too long to choose a winner you could try reducing the X number in line 9∅ to something like 13∅, and changing line 1∅∅ to read:

    1∅∅ FOR D = 1 TO X/4

This is a good program to experiment with.

Program 2. *** AVERAGES ***

```
1∅ PRINT "*** AVERAGES ***"
2∅ LET C = ∅
3∅ LET T = ∅
4∅ PRINT "THIS PROGRAM WILL WORK OUT THE"
5∅ PRINT "AVERAGE OF THE NUMBERS INPUT."
6∅ PRINT "FINISH OFF YOUR INPUT LIST"
7∅ PRINT "WITH THE NUMBER 99999."
8∅ INPUT N
9∅ IF N = 99999 THEN GOTO 13∅
1∅∅ LET C = C + 1
11∅ LET T = T + N
12∅ GOTO 8∅
13∅ PRINT "THE AVERAGE IS  "; T/C
14∅ END
```

This is a very simple program which counts how many numbers you INPUT at line 8∅ and keeps the total of these numbers at line 11∅. The average is then calculated and PRINTed by line 13∅.

Program 3. *** DICE ***

```
1∅ PRINT "*** DICE ***"
2∅ PRINT "DO YOU WANT ONE OR"
```

```
  3Ø PRINT "TWO DICE TO THROW?"
 3ØØ INPUT N
 4ØØ IF N <> 1 AND N <> 2 THEN GOTO 2Ø
 6ØØ PRINT
 61Ø PRINT
 63Ø PRINT
 64Ø PRINT
 65Ø PRINT "PRESS T TO THROW"
 7ØØ INPUT T$
 75Ø REM OPTIONAL CLEAR SCREEN
 8ØØ PRINT
 9ØØ PRINT
1ØØØ FOR R = 1 TO N STEP 1
1Ø5Ø IF R = 2 THEN PRINT "- - - - - - - - - -"
11ØØ REM RANDOM NUMBER FROM 1 TO 6
12ØØ LET D = INT (RND(X) * 6) + 1
14ØØ IF D = 2 THEN GOTO 3ØØØ
15ØØ IF D = 3 THEN GOTO 4ØØØ
16ØØ IF D = 4 THEN GOTO 5ØØØ
17ØØ IF D = 5 THEN GOTO 6ØØØ
18ØØ IF D = 6 THEN GOTO 7ØØØ
2ØØØ GOSUB 9Ø8Ø
2Ø1Ø GOSUB 9Ø6Ø
2Ø2Ø GOSUB 9Ø8Ø
2Ø25 NEXT R
2Ø3Ø GOTO 6ØØ
3ØØØ GOSUB 9Ø2Ø
3Ø1Ø GOSUB 9Ø8Ø
3Ø2Ø GOSUB 9Ø4Ø
3Ø25 NEXT R
3Ø3Ø GOTO 6ØØ
4ØØØ GOSUB 9Ø2Ø
4Ø1Ø GOSUB 9Ø6Ø
4Ø2Ø GOSUB 9Ø4Ø
4Ø25 NEXT R
4Ø3Ø GOTO 6ØØ
5ØØØ GOSUB 9ØØØ
5Ø1Ø GOSUB 9Ø8Ø
5Ø2Ø GOSUB 9ØØØ
5Ø25 NEXT R
5Ø3Ø GOTO 6ØØ
6ØØØ GOSUB 9ØØØ
6Ø1Ø GOSUB 9Ø6Ø
6Ø2Ø GOSUB 9ØØØ
6Ø25 NEXT R
```

```
6030 GOTO 600
7000 GOSUB 9000
7010 GOSUB 9000
7020 GOSUB 9000
7025 NEXT R
7030 GOTO 600
9000 PRINT "    XX    XX"
9010 RETURN
9020 PRINT "    XX        "
9030 RETURN
9040 PRINT "          XX"
9050 RETURN
9060 PRINT "       XX     "
9070 RETURN
9080 PRINT "              "
9090 RETURN
```

This is a long program which makes use of GOSUBs to build up a picture of one, or two, dice. Line 1200 chooses a number at RaNDom and lines 1400 – 1800 send the computer to the special section which chooses which of the lines from 9000 to 9090 are needed to form the picture of the dice. If you ask for two dice to be thrown, the FOR . . . NEXT loop at line 1000 sends the computer through the program a second time. Make sure that you enter lines 9000 – 9080 into your computer correctly. We must admit that we could have made a better job of drawing the dice on the screen — we shall leave it to you to make the improvement!

Program 4. *** RUSSIAN ROULETTE ***

```
10 PRINT "*** RUSSIAN ROULETTE ***"
20 GOSUB 3000
50 PRINT "INPUT 6 NAMES PLEASE"
60 INPUT B$
61 INPUT C$
62 INPUT D$
63 INPUT E$
64 INPUT F$
65 INPUT G$
70 GOSUB 4000
71 REM OPTIONALLY REPLACE LINE 70 WITH CLEAR
   SCREEN STATEMENT
80 LET X = 0
90 LET C = INT (RND(X) * 6) + 1
105 PRINT
110 PRINT "NOW "; B$;" PUT A BULLET INTO"
120 PRINT "THE GUN — SPIN THE CHAMBER"
```

```
130 PRINT "AND POINT IT AT YOUR HEAD."
140  PRINT "TO PULL THE TRIGGER PRESS T"
160 LET N$ = B$
170 GOSUB 5000
190 LET N$ = C$
200 GOSUB 4000
210 PRINT "NOW IT IS YOUR TURN "; C$
230 GOSUB 5000
250 LET N$ = D$
260 GOSUB 4000
261 REM OPTIONALLY REPLACE LINE 260 WITH CLEAR
    SCREEN STATEMENT
270 PRINT D$ ;", IT IS YOUR TURN NOW"
280 GOSUB 5000
300 LET N$ = E$
310 GOSUB 4000
311 REM OPTIONALLY REPLACE LINE 310 WITH CLEAR
    SCREEN STATEMENT
320 PRINT "DO NOT SHAKE SO MUCH "; E$
340 GOSUB 5000
360 LET N$ = F$
370 GOSUB 4000
371 REM OPTIONALLY REPLACE LINE 370 WITH CLEAR
    SCREEN STATEMENT
380 PRINT "SAFE SO FAR — EXCEPT PERHAPS"
```

```
390 PRINT "FOR YOU "; F$
410 GOSUB 5000
430 LET N$ = G$
432 PRINT
434 PRINT
436 PRINT
440 PRINT "IT IS NOT YOUR LUCKY DAY "; G$
450 PRINT "I WILL PULL THE TRIGGER FOR YOU."
452 PRINT
```

```
 454 PRINT
 456 PRINT
 460 FOR R = 1 TO 1500 STEP 1
 470 NEXT R
 480 GOTO 2000
2000 PRINT "XXX . . . XX . . X . . X . . XXX "
2001 PRINT "X . . X . X . . X . XX . X . X "
2002 PRINT "X . . X . X . . X . XX . X . X "
2003 PRINT "XXX . . XXXX . XXXX . X . X XX "
2004 PRINT "X . . X . X . . X . X . XX . X . . X "
2005 PRINT "X . . X . X . . X . X . XX . X . . X "
2006 PRINT "XXX . . X . . X . X . . X . . XX"
2008 PRINT
2009 PRINT
2010 PRINT "SORRY   "; N$; "   YOU ARE DEAD"
2020 FOR R = 1 TO 1000 STEP 1
2030 NEXT R
2050 PRINT
2051 REM OPTIONAL CLEAR SCREEN
2060 PRINT
2070 PRINT "DO THOSE OF YOU LEFT WANT"
2080 PRINT "ANOTHER GO? (YES OR NO)"
2090 INPUT A$
2100 PRINT
2110 PRINT
2120 IF A$ = "YES" THEN GOTO 2145
2130 PRINT "THANK YOU FOR THE GAME"
2140 END
2145 PRINT
2148 PRINT
2150 PRINT "FOR NEW NAMES, PRESS 1"
2180 PRINT
2200 PRINT
2210 PRINT "FOR SAME PEOPLE AGAIN, PRESS 2"
2220 PRINT "   "; N$; "   WILL COME BACK TO LIFE"
2250 INPUT C
2260 IF C = 1 THEN GOTO 50
2265 GOSUB 4000
2266 REM OPTIONALLY REPLACE LINE 2265 WITH A CLEAR
     SCREEN STATEMENT
2270 GOTO 80
3000 PRINT
```

```
3020 PRINT " IXXXXXXXXXXXXXXXXXXXXK"
3030 PRINT " . . . . IXXXOOOOOOOOXXXI"
3040 PRINT " . . . . . .MOOOOOOOOXXXI"
3050 PRINT " . . . . . .MOOOOOOOOXM"
3060 PRINT " . . . . . . . . ) . IX XXXXXXI"
3070 PRINT " . . . . . . . . . . IX XXXXXXI"
3080 PRINT " . . . . . . . . . . .MXXXXM"
3090 PRINT " . . . . . . . . . . .MXXXXM"
3100 PRINT
3120 RETURN
4000 FOR R = 1 TO 20 STEP 1
4010 PRINT
4020 NEXT R
4030 RETURN
5000 INPUT T$
5010 LET X = X + 1
5020 GOSUB 3000
5030 FOR R = 1 TO 1000 STEP 1
5040 NEXT R
5050 IF X = C THEN GOTO 2000
5060 PRINT
5070 PRINT
5080 PRINT " . . . CLICK . . ."
5090 PRINT "YOU ARE SAFE"
5100 FOR R = 1 TO 1000 STEP 1
5110 NEXT R
5120 RETURN
```

This is the longest program in the whole book. However, most of
the lines are short and easy to understand. Make sure that you enter
lines 2000 - 2006 correctly, and also lines 3020 - 3090. Don't enter
the full stops — they are there to show you how many spaces to
type. Once again GOSUBs are extensively used. Note how the
name of the person holding the gun is stored in N$ by the lines 160,
190, 250 etc. This is so that the correct name may be brought back
to life by line 2220. To speed up the game, try reducing the R values
in lines 460, 2020, 5030 and 5100.

Once you have RUN these programs we hope that you will try to
improve them. This is what we would like you to do! Don't forget,
you can SAVE these programs once they are put into the computer
so if you really make a mess of changing them you can always go
back to square one by LOADing the original programs again.

16

DATA, READ and RESTORE statements

Up to now, we have given values to the computer's memory boxes either by using a LET statement like this:

10 LET A = 5

or by using an INPUT statement like this:

30 INPUT A

Now we shall look at another method of giving values to memory boxes using three new keywords called DATA, READ and RESTORE. These will enable us to write program lines which will enter lots of values into memory boxes without having to use separate LET or INPUT statements for each value.

(Some computers do not use DATA, READ and RESTORE statements. If yours is one of these we suggest you skip this chapter and go straight on to Chapter 17.)

Have a look at this program:

10 DATA 3,4,5,6,7,8
20 READ A,B
30 PRINT A + B
40 GOTO 20

Line 10 contains DATA (information) for the program to use. When the program is RUN, line 20 tells the computer to READ the DATA. As there are two memory box names, A and B, the computer READs two pieces of DATA. The first two pieces of DATA in line 10 are the numbers 3 and 4 so the computer READs them and puts their values into the two memory boxes --- 3 into A and 4 into B. Line 30 then tells the computer to PRINT A + B which of course is 7.

Line 40 now tells the computer to GOTO 20 where it is again told to READ two pieces of DATA. The computer remembers how far along the line of DATA it has read (clever things these computers!),

so now it READs the next two pieces of DATA which are the numbers 5 and 6. The computer now gives these values to memory boxes A and B in place of the old values, and then PRINTs them added together --- 11. Then it goes back to line 2Ø and does the same thing again with the numbers 7 and 8. So by now it has PRINTed three numbers on the screen:

                7 (three plus four)
              11 (five plus six)
       and 15 (seven plus eight)

The next time the computer loops round to line 2Ø there are no numbers left to READ in the DATA line. When this happens, the program immediately stops RUNning and the computer PRINTs an error message on the screen. This message may say something like:

    OUT OF DATA IN 1Ø

or it may be much shorter; the exact message will differ from computer to computer. Now try RUNning the program to see firstly, if it works in the way we said it would and secondly, what sort of error message your own computer gives.

Here is another program to try:

```
1Ø DATA 5,3,8,6,4,2,999
2Ø LET A = Ø
3Ø READ N
4Ø IF N = 999 THEN END
5Ø PRINT A; "  PLUS  "; N; "  EQUALS  "; A + N
6Ø LET A = A + N
7Ø GOTO 3Ø
```

Before you RUN this program, try to work out for yourself what the program is designed to do. You will see the line of DATA in line

1∅, and the statement at line 3∅ to READ it into memory box N. This time there is only one memory box mentioned in line 3∅ so the computer will only READ one piece of DATA at a time, instead of two.

Now RUN the program and check what the computer does. You will see that it adds the items of DATA together one by one and PRINTs out the answers as it goes along. The PRINTing and adding take place in line 5∅, and memory box A is updated with the running total in line 6∅. The computer then loops back to READ the next item of DATA.

Did the computer give you an error message this time when it ran out of DATA? It shouldn't have done because of the special DATA item we put at the end of line 1∅ (999) and the IF THEN statement in line 4∅ which tells the computer to END if the last number it has read (and put into memory box N) is 999. This is how we can make sure that a program using DATA and READ statements ENDs properly instead of just stopping with an error message. Of course you must make sure that the special number you use is not going to be an item of DATA that you want the computer to READ and use in your program. In other programs, you may want to tell the computer to GOTO a separate part of the program once it has read all the DATA. You would do this with an IF THEN statement like the one we have used, but instead of saying 'END' you would say 'GOTO' and the first line number of the new part of your program.

If you wanted the computer to READ the line of DATA more than once in a program you would use the third keyword we are introducing in this chapter — RESTORE. RESTORE tells the computer to start again at the beginning of the DATA line when it is next told to do a READ. To check how it works, add these extra lines to the previous program:

    8∅ RESTORE
    9∅ GOTO 2∅

and change line 4∅ to read:

    4∅ IF N = 999 THEN GOTO 8∅

Now RUN the program again. It should just keep on looping until you stop it by pressing the BREAK or CONTROL and C keys. Now change line 8∅ to read:

    8∅ GOTO 2∅

Now RUN the program again and check that without RESTORE it will only work once before it gives you its OUT OF DATA message.

Up to now we have spoken only about READing numbers from DATA statements. It is of course also possible to READ words from

DATA statements. To show you how, type in this program:

```
1Ø DATA HELEN, PHILIP, WILLIAM, CLARE, PENNY, STOP
2Ø READ N$
3Ø IF N$ = "STOP" THEN END
4Ø PRINT N$
5Ø GOTO 2Ø
```

RUN it to prove that it works just as the numbers one did. Did you notice that this program READs and PRINTs using a $ memory box (a string variable)?

You can also mix words with numbers in the DATA line:

```
1Ø DATA HELEN, 15, PHILIP, 12, WILLIAM, 1Ø
2Ø DATA CLARE, 9, PENNY, 8, STOP, 999
3Ø READ N$, A
4Ø IF N$ = "STOP" AND A = 999 THEN END
5Ø PRINT N$,A
6Ø GOTO 3Ø
```

This time, we have added the people's ages next to their names in the DATA lines and have PRINTed them out side-by-side. Note that in this program we have more DATA than will fit on to a single line. The computer will READ the DATA just as if it is all one long line of DATA.

Later in this book we will show you a more complex program built up round this type of DATA statement.

17

Arrays

The names of the memory boxes we have used so far have had single letters:

A,B,E, etc., to hold numbers (numerical);
A$,B$,E$, etc., to hold any characters (alphanumeric).

As there are only 26 letters in the alphabet, this means that the maximum number of memory boxes available for use in programs would be 52 (26 numerical and 26 alphanumeric). In the programs we have been writing up to now, this has been adequate, but when we start writing more complicated programs we may find that more will be needed.

To give us more memory boxes we can put numbers after the letters like this:

A1, A2, A3, B6, E9, etc.

We can use all the numbers up to nine including zero. This gives us a further ten memory boxes for each letter, making a total of 11 memory boxes for each letter.

Here are all the numerical memory boxes for the letter A:

A, AØ, A1, A2, A3, A4, A5, A6, A7, A8, A9

and the alphanumeric ones:

A$, AØ$, A1$, A2$, A3$, A4$, A5$, A6$, A7$, A8$, A9$

So now we have 286 (26 times 11) numerical memory boxes and the same number of alphanumeric.

In addition to these, instead of a number after the first letter, some computers allow us to use another letter like this:

AA, AB, AC, EA, EB, AA$, AB$.

Some computers even let us use full words like these:

BUS
CARS
TRAINS
JANE

so we could then have statements looking like these:

1Ø LET AB = 2Ø
2Ø LET BUS = 1Ø
3Ø LET TRAINS = 42
4Ø LET DIANE = 25

Your own computer's manual will tell you which type of memory boxes your computer will allow.

You can see that by using these different methods we can now have the use of a large number of memory boxes. However, this is not the end of the matter because there is yet another type of memory box called an 'ARRAY'. This is a big memory box which can be split up into smaller compartments. You can think of an array as being like one floor in a block of flats. This is a diagram of a block of flats, which has five floors; A, B, C, D and E:

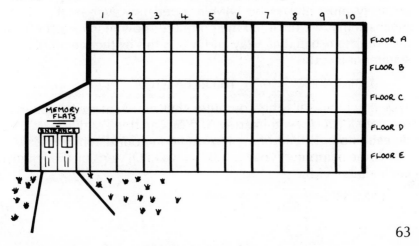

There are ten flats on each floor and the floors have been given letters (A, B, C etc). If you wanted to send a parcel to floor B, flat 3 you could address your parcel like this:

B 3

and that would be sufficient for the postman to know which flat you meant. You could write the address of any of the flats like that and the postman should always find the correct one.

It is just the same with the computer's arrays. The only difference is that we put brackets round the numbers like this:

A(1), A(2), E(3), G(9) etc.

The numbers in brackets are the memory box compartments we mentioned earlier and are called subscripts.

If we are going to use more than 10 separate subscripts in any one array, we must DIMension the array first. (With certain computers, an array must always be DIMensioned however small). All this means is that we must tell the computer how many subscripts we are going to use in that array and we do this by the means of a DIM statement like this:

1Ø DIM A(1ØØ)   or   1Ø DIM A$(1ØØ)

This statement tells the computer that we want to set aside 1ØØ separate locations within array A. (You can think of that as 1ØØ flats on each floor instead of the ten we had in our diagram).

In some computers you may also have to DIMension the length of each alpha field, e.g.:

DIM A$(5,1Ø)

This will provide five locations of up to 1Ø characters each and we shall be meeting this type of array in the next chapter.

In the following program we shall use an array 'A' which will have 4 memory compartments. The program adds 3 numbers together then PRINTS the answer. Enter and RUN this program to assure yourself that arrays behave just like ordinary memory boxes.

```
 5 DIM A(4)
1Ø LET A(1) = 35
2Ø LET A(2) = 16
3Ø LET A(3) = 12
4Ø LET A(4) = A(1) + A(2) + A(3)
5Ø PRINT A(4)
6Ø END
```

In our diagram, we have only shown 10 flats on each floor. In the computer's memory there may be as many as 250 or more locations available for each letter so we could have memory boxes looking like these:

A(89), Z(234), BQ(79), A3(254)

In addition to these numerical memory boxes we can also have alphanumeric ones like these:

A$(89), Z$(234), BQ$(79), A3$(254)

We don't have to use numbers as the subscripts (the characters in the brackets). If we wanted to, we could put other memory box addresses in, like these:

A(D), A$(P), etc.

Type in this small program and RUN it:

```
 5 DIM A(4Ø)
1Ø LET D = 39
2Ø LET A(D) = 111111
3Ø PRINT A(39)
```

We could have put 39 as the subscript in line 2Ø, but instead we put D. When the computer reached line 2Ø, it saw that it had to put 111111 into memory location A(D). It knew from line 1Ø that D = 39, so it put 111111 into A(39). Line 3Ø then PRINTed out the 111111 from that memory cell. In most programs you will see letters as subscripts rather than numbers.

18

Using array subscripts

Now that you have been introduced to ARRAYS and SUBSCRIPTS and have an idea how they work, we shall take a further look at them and make use of them. You will find that experienced programmers make great use of arrays even though they could often have used the ordinary (A and A$, etc.) variables instead. This is because it is very easy to put data into arrays and even easier to select particular memory boxes using subscripts.

To put information or data into an array, we can use simple LET statements as we did in Chapter 17, or we could use INPUT statements like this:

```
 5 DIM N$(5, 1Ø)
 6 DIM A(5)
1Ø FOR R = 1 TO 5 STEP 1
2Ø INPUT N$(R)
3Ø INPUT A(R)
4Ø NEXT R
```

This program will enable us to put information into 5 alphanumeric memory locations N$(1) to N$(5), and also numbers into 5 numerical memory locations A(1) to A(5).

Use this program to INPUT the names of 5 of your friends into array N$ and their ages into array A, and then PRINT out the names and ages of your choice. Do you remember how to do this? Just PRINT out the array subscripts in immediate mode like this:

```
    PRINT N$(5)
 or PRINT A(2) etc.
```

Now that these arrays have been set up with data, you could continue with further program lines from line 5Ø onwards, and make use of the data they contain.

Some computers allow yet another method of putting values into an array by using a FOR NEXT STEP loop. Here is a sample program which sets up two arrays, putting alphanumeric data into one array and numerical data into the other:

```
5 REM YOU MAY NEED TO DIM YOUR ARRAY
1∅ DATA HELEN, 15, PHILIP, 12, WILLIAM, 1∅
2∅ DATA CLARE, 9, PENNY, 8
3∅ FOR R = 1 TO 5 STEP 1
4∅ READ N$(R),A(R)
5∅ NEXT R
6∅ (rest of program)
```

You may recognise this DATA as being the same as that we used in the program at the end of Chapter 16. This program is shorter than the program we used then but it does the same job — and more! We have used a FOR NEXT STEP loop to READ the 5 names and ages, which means we no longer need STOP, 999 and IF THEN statements. Also, by using the variable R to increase the subscript by one each time the computer loops round, we are able to READ the DATA into separate memory locations within the array.

The original program in Chapter 16 PRINTed each name and age in turn, but the only ones actually left in the two memory boxes when the program had finished RUNning were 'PENNY' in N$ and '8' in A. This time however, all the names and ages are held in separate memory locations so we could use them in any following program that we might care to write.

We shall now use many of the ideas we have mentioned in a program which we shall call, 'THE RUDE PROGRAM'. Here is the program listing:

```
 5 DIM B$ (11,9)
 6 DIM A$ (5,8)
 7 DIM N$ (6,1∅)
1∅ REM RUDE PROGRAM
2∅ DATA BLUE, BLACK, RED, ORANGE
3∅ DATA PINK, ROUND, UGLY, POINTED
4∅ DATA BEAUTIFUL, BENT, SPIKY
5∅ DATA LOVES, HATES, ADORES
6∅ DATA WORSHIPS, SO HAS
7∅ FOR R = 1 TO 11 STEP 1
8∅ READ B$(R)
9∅ NEXT R
1∅∅ FOR S = 1 TO 5 STEP 1
11∅ READ A$(S)
12∅ NEXT S
```

```
13Ø PRINT "INPUT 6 NAMES"
14Ø FOR T = 1 TO 6 STEP 1
15Ø INPUT N$(T)
16Ø NEXT T
165 REM OPTIONAL CLEAR SCREEN
17Ø PRINT
18Ø PRINT
19Ø LET D = INT (RND(X) * 6) + 1
195 REM RANDOM NUMBER FROM 1 TO 6
2ØØ LET E = INT (RND (X) * 11) + 1
21Ø LET F = INT(RND(X) * 11) + 1
22Ø LET G = INT(RND(X) * 11) + 1
225 REM RANDOM NUMBERS FROM 1 TO 11
23Ø LET H = INT(RND(X) * 5) + 1
235 REM RANDOM NUMBER FROM 1 TO 5
24Ø LET J = INT(RND(X) * 6) + 1
245 REM RANDOM NUMBER FROM 1 TO 6
25Ø PRINT N$(D); " HAS "; B$(E); " HAIR  AND "; B$(F)
26Ø PRINT "EYES AND A "; B$(G); " NOSE"
27Ø PRINT " AND "; A$(H);" "; N$(J)
28Ø PRINT
29Ø PRINT
3ØØ PRINT "FOR NEW NAMES, PRESS 1."
31Ø PRINT "FOR THE SAME AGAIN, PRESS 2."
32Ø PRINT
33Ø INPUT P
34Ø IF P = 1 THEN GOTO 13Ø
35Ø GOTO 19Ø
```

Most computers can use DATA, READ and RESTORE statements.
If your computer is not one of these, we suggest you change some of
the program lines like this:

2Ø, 3Ø, 4Ø, 5Ø and 6Ø will not be needed.
Change 8Ø to: 8Ø   INPUT B$(R)
Change 11Ø to: 11Ø   INPUT A$(S)

When you RUN the program, just INPUT the eleven words in
lines 2Ø, 3Ø and 4Ø and then the words in lines 5Ø and 6Ø, but do not
INPUT the word 'DATA'!

This is quite a long program, but we think you will find it worth the
effort of typing it in as it should give you plenty of amusement! Try to
understand what each line will do as you type it in. Also see if you
can spot any routines that would work by themselves.

When the program asks you for six names, enter the names of six
of your friends or family. The program will use these names,

together with the words in the DATA lines 2∅ to 6∅, to set up three arrays:

A$(1) to A$(5)
B$(1) to B$(11)
N$(1) to N$(6)

When this is done, the program will PRINT a sentence (lines 25∅ to 27∅), filling in the gaps by selecting various memory locations (using subscripts) at RaNDom. To explain how this works let's look at line 25∅ which will PRINT:

(someone) HAS (???) HAIR AND (???)

Which 'someone' will depend on the RaNDom number D used as a subscript by line 25∅. If D were a 2, then N$(2) would be PRINTed. Likewise, with the first (???) which is B$(E). If the RaNDom number for E were, say, a 4, then memory location B$(4) would be PRINTed which would be ORANGE. Exactly the same thing happens with the RaNDom number F for the third gap. The computer will tell you things about your friends and family which you may not have known before!

You may not like our choice of words in this program. Why not experiment with some words of your own? You could even experiment with a 'nice' program and be even ruder than we have been!

This is the last chapter in which we shall introduce new keywords so we suggest that you make the effort to alter not only this program, but any of our others if you feel that you would like to. The more you experiment, the sooner you will become a good programmer.

The chapters up to now have been written to teach you how to program a computer. The following chapters will help you to become a better programmer; we suggest you read them carefully and do all of the programs.

19

Useful routines

This chapter consists of several subroutines which you may find useful when you begin writing programs of your own. You will probably recognise some of the routines from programs earlier in the book but we think it will be useful for you to have them all together in one chapter for reference purposes.

1.   COUNTER

You may find that you need to keep a count of how many times a particular line, or sequence of lines, is executed during a RUN of a program. If, for instance, you wanted to know how many times line 3Ø in the following example is executed you could put your counter in the line next to it (line 2Ø). Later in your program, when you would have said GOTO 3Ø, you say instead GOTO 2Ø. Memory box X will then hold the number of times line 3Ø had been executed:

    1Ø LET X = Ø
    2Ø LET X = X + 1

```
3Ø (program line to be counted)
4Ø (rest of program)
12Ø (rest of program)
13Ø GOTO 2Ø
```

This counter could be used for:

counting questions asked in a game;
counting the number of correct answers;
counting the number of wrong answers, etc.

2. TIME DELAY

You may want to display a message on the screen only just long enough for someone to read, or perhaps delay PRINTing something to build up suspense as we did in the RUSSIAN ROULETTE program in Chapter 15. You could use a routine like this at the point where you want the delay:

```
1Ø FOR R = 1 TO 1ØØØ STEP 1
2Ø NEXT R
```

The program will loop between these two lines until R becomes 1ØØØ. This will delay the execution of the rest of the program. To increase the delay you could change the 1ØØØ to 5ØØØ, or even 1ØØØØ.

3. ANOTHER TIME DELAY

This you would use if you wanted to stop the program until someone uses the keyboard:

3Ø INPUT Q7$ (or any variable not used elsewhere in the program)

When the computer reaches line 3Ø it will ask for INPUT into the keyboard. Any key (then RETURN) that is pressed will then allow the rest of the program to be executed. You won't mind which key is pressed because you will not be using the variable Q7$ in your program calculations. This type of delay is most useful when you have more lines to PRINT than will fit on the screen at one time. This could be the case in a games program, for instance, where the instructions on how to play the game take up 20 PRINT lines but your screen can perhaps display only 16 lines at any one time. You would place your INPUT statement after, say, the tenth PRINTed line so that the reader can continue with the remaining 10 lines when he is ready, by entering any character and pressing RETURN.

4. CLEAR SCREEN

This routine PRINTs 40 blank lines so that the screen is cleared by the program:

```
1Ø FOR R = 1 TO 4Ø STEP 1
2Ø PRINT
3Ø NEXT R
```

Please note: you only need as many loops as you have lines on your screen. You might use a clear screen statement.

5. ROUNDING

Answers to calculations will often be given to many places of decimals, looking something like this: 4·831674. In many instances, this may be perfectly acceptable but supposing you wanted the answer to be to the nearest whole number? If you were just to take the INTeger part of the number, the answer would be given as 4. However, the nearest whole number in this case is 5. We get over this problem by adding ·5 and taking the INTeger of the total, like this:

```
1Ø LET A = INT(A + ·5)
```

Now, if the decimal part of your answer is greater than ·5 then A will be given the value of the next highest INTeger. If the decimal part is less than ·5 the answer will just be the whole number part of the answer. Here are some examples of numbers with decimal parts both before and after rounding by line 1Ø:

BEFORE	AFTER
438·762	439·
4·38	4·
12·ØØ1	12·
18·9999	19·
4·5	5·

If you prefer numbers like 4·5 to be rounded to 4 rather than 5 then change line 1∅ to read:

1∅ LET A = INT(A + ·4999)

6. SORTING

Sometimes you may need to sort a list of numbers into amount order. Here is a routine that will do this for you. It sorts the numbers into increasing value order, i.e. the smallest number first.

```
1∅ DATA 21,46,12,16,1∅,94,36,21
2∅ FOR R = 1 TO 8 STEP 1
3∅ READ A(R)
4∅ NEXT R
5∅ FOR S = 1 TO 8 STEP 1
6∅ FOR T = ∅ TO 7 STEP 1
7∅ IF A (T + 1) >= A(T) THEN GOTO 11∅
8∅ LET D = A(T)
9∅ LET A(T) = A(T + 1)
1∅∅ LET A(T + 1) = D
11∅ NEXT T
12∅ NEXT S
13∅ REM THE FOLLOWING LINES PROVE THE PROGRAM
    WORKS
14∅ FOR R = 1 TO 8 STEP 1
15∅ PRINT A(R)
16∅ NEXT R
```

The DATA is all read into the A array which in this particular program has 8 locations. You could use INPUT statements to fill the array if you wish, by deleting line 1∅ and changing line 3∅ to read 3∅ INPUT A(R).

Lines 5∅ and 6∅ look at the first two locations. If the first number is less than or equal to the second one, it leaves them in order and then compares the second and third numbers in the same way. It continues to compare until it finds a number which is smaller. Lines

8Ø, 9Ø and 1ØØ swap these two numbers round before comparing the next two in the list. Gradually, all the numbers in the list are swapped until the last number in the array (memory location A(8)) is the highest number. Then the program repeats the sequence another seven times until all the numbers are in order.

7. CONTROL OF INPUT

Here is a simple routine which will limit what is INPUT into memory box N:

    1Ø INPUT N
    2Ø IF N < 1 OR N > 1ØØ THEN GOTO 1Ø

You are only allowed to INPUT a number from 1 to 1ØØ (but you can of course change the numbers to suit your own program).

8. PASSWORD CONTROL

This routine asks you for a password. If you enter the password correctly, the routine sends the computer on to the rest of the program (which starts at line 6Ø). In this particular program, if you enter the wrong password, not only does the routine prevent you going on to the rest of the program, but line 5Ø clears out the program from your computer's memory with the word NEW! This prevents someone from reading the listing of your program to see what the password is!

    1Ø PRINT "ENTER PASSWORD"
    2Ø INPUT P$
    3Ø IF P$ = "BATMAN" THEN GOTO 6Ø
    4Ø PRINT "ACCESS DENIED"
    5Ø NEW
    6Ø (rest of program)

These are just a few of the many routines that may be used. You will find many more in programs that you meet in the future. We suggest that you make a note of those you think you will be able to use in your own programs.

20

Debugging programs

Computer programs have to be exactly right if they are to work properly. You have probably found this out already if you have made mistakes when typing our programs into your computer! Even expert programmers make errors when writing programs. In fact, it is unusual for programs to work first time; there are nearly always some little things (or maybe big things!) wrong with them when they are first written. Errors in a computer program are called 'bugs'.

There are two types of errors which can be made when writing programs. These are SYNTAX errors and LOGIC errors.

A syntax error is an error in the way a statement is written, such as a word spelt wrongly:

IPNUT (should be INPUT)
GO TO (should be one word GOTO)

or perhaps a PRINT statement like this:

PRINT GOOD MORNING (the quotation marks are missing)

Some computers will not allow syntax errors; as soon as you press the RETURN key after typing a statement containing a syntax error, these computers give you an error message and will not allow you to type another line until you have corrected the statement. Other computers will allow you to enter the statement incorrectly, but the program will stop when it gets to the incorrect line and the computer will print an error message.

A logic error is a mistake in telling the computer what to do. The statements are written correctly but they tell the computer to do the wrong things! Some logic errors will stop a program from RUNning, while others will make a program RUN incorrectly and give you the wrong answers or just a lot of rubbish. Examples of logic errors are:

- telling the computer to add the wrong variables together;
- a GOTO statement telling the computer to GOTO the wrong line number.

Here are some more examples of errors (both syntax and logic errors), which people commonly make when writing programs:

- a NEXT statement with no FOR statement;
- a RETURN statement with no GOSUB statement;
- using an array with more than 1∅ subscripts which has not been DIMensioned;
- trying to divide a number by zero;
- an IF statement without a THEN;
- trying to GOTO a line number which does not exist;
- trying to PRINT too many lines on a screen (some of the PRINTing disappears off the top of the screen);
- an IF statement where the condition can never be true, for example:

```
1∅ LET X = 1
2∅ LET X = X + 2
3∅ IF X = 3∅ THEN GOTO 18∅
4∅ GOTO 2∅
```

In this program, X will never equal 30 because it starts with a value of 1 and increases by two each time the program loops back to line 2∅. The nearest X gets to a value of 30 will be 29 or 31. The IF statement in line 3∅ could have read:

```
3∅ IF X > 3∅ THEN GOTO 18∅
or 3∅ IF X = 31 THEN GOTO 18∅
```

Something else that often gives trouble is a statement that contains more than one piece of arithmetic, like this:

76

```
1∅ LET B = 2
2∅ LET C = 4
3∅ LET A = B * C + 2
```

You may already realise that there are two possible values for A depending upon how the computer does the calculation in line 3∅. If the computer was first to multiply B by C and then add 2, the answer would be:

2 * 4 = 8 then 8 + 2 equals 10

But if the computer did the addition first, the answer would be:

4 + 2 = 6 then 6 * 2 equals 12

In fact computers always do multiplication and division (* and /) before they do addition and subtraction (+ and –). So, in the above example, A would be given the value of 10. You could, if you wanted to, change the order by using brackets like this:

```
3∅ LET A = B * (C + 2)
```

The computer will do whatever is in the brackets before it does anything else. So it will first add C and 2 together, and will then multiply the answer by B. The value of A will then be 12. If you have any doubts about the order in which your computer will do some calculations, the safest thing is to split the calculations up and put them on separate lines. For instance, line 3∅ above could be written like this:

```
3∅ LET A = C + 2
35 LET A = B * A
```

In this way, you can be sure that your sums are computed in the right order.

MANY PROGRAMMING ERRORS CAN BE AVOIDED BY THINKING CAREFULLY ABOUT A PROGRAM BEFORE STARTING TO WRITE IT.

Write down all the steps of the program before you start. The important thing to do is to work out the FLOW of the program — how you are going to achieve what you want the computer to do for you, and the steps you think the computer will need to take to achieve your goal.

Turn back to the number guessing game in Chapter 9. Before we wrote the program, we noted down all the steps we thought would be necessary for the program to work, and decided on the FLOW of the program rather like this.

1. PRINT a message asking for a number between 1 and 1∅∅.
2. Have an INPUT statement to accept the INPUT into memory box N.

3. PRINT a message asking for the person to enter his guess.
4. Have an INPUT statement accept the guess into memory box G.
5. If G is less than the number, tell him and ask him to try again.
6. If G is higher, tell him and ask him to try again.
7. Go back and wait for another number.
8. If G is correct, tell him.

Having decided on the FLOW of the program in this way, it was quite an easy matter actually to write the program.

Another way of writing down the flow of a program is by drawing a FLOWCHART. A flowchart consists of lots of boxes of various shapes connected by lines which you draw to help you to understand how the program will RUN. We shall not be going into flowcharts in this book; there are various books on the subject which you might like to read at a later date.

If all the programs you write work perfectly first time, every time, you are a brilliant programmer who should go to the very top in the world of computers. If (like us!) you have some problems with the programs you write, you will probably need to spend some time getting new programs to work perfectly. The process of testing programs and finding and correcting bugs is called debugging. Here are a few tips on getting programs to work, (you may find them useful when you get on to the next chapter!):

1. If your program asks for a RaNDom number, put in an INPUT statement so that you can force a particular number into the variable A while you are testing the program. Here is an example:

```
40 LET A = RND(X)
41 INPUT A
50 (rest of the program)
```

We have added line 41 while we test the program so that we can always be sure of the value of A. As soon as the program is running correctly, we shall remove line 41.

2. To check that calculations are being performed as you would expect them to be, insert statements to PRINT the values of the variables at particular points in a program:

e.g. 41 PRINT "AT LINE 41, B = "; B
or   52 PRINT "AT LINE 52, X = "; X

3. Statements similar to those in 2 above can be used after RND statements to make sure that the computer is providing numbers in the range you expect. Once again, you would remove the statements in the finished program.

4. You could leave the RANDOMIZE statement out of a program during testing so that you know what the RND number will be.

5. After each routine you could put in a STOP statement (just the line number and the word STOP). The program will then stop running and you will be able to check (or change) the values of any variables in immediate mode. To make the program continue running, you type CONT and the program will just carry on from where it left off.

6. Check the computer's arithmetic with a calculator to make sure that it is working out its answers in the way that you meant it to.

7. Check the spelling and punctuation in all the statements to make sure that you have not left out any quotation marks or put in commas instead of semicolons, etc.

8. Check conditional statements (IF THEN) by putting values into memory boxes so that both the true and untrue conditions are satisfactorily tested. You can do this by inserting an INPUT statement before the IF THEN as in 1 above.

Now have a go at correcting the programs in Chapter 21 and getting them to work properly.

GOOD LUCK!

21

Some debugging exercises

This is where we see how good you are at debugging programs! In this chapter you will find several short programs and each one has at least one error in it. Your job is to find the errors and get the programs RUNning properly. To assist you in your efforts we shall, of course, tell you what the programs are supposed to do! You will probably find a lot of the errors simply by reading the programs. To find the rest, type the programs into your computer, then RUN them and check the results. It is important to do this because there are some errors that you may not find unless you do! If you have any problems, you will find the solutions in Appendix 1.

Program 1
This program asks you to INPUT a number. It then multiplies that number by 5 and PRINTs the answer.

```
1Ø INPUT A
2Ø LET B = A * 5
3Ø PRINT "B"
4Ø END
```

Program 2
This program asks you to INPUT a number. It then tells you whether your number is less than 5, or 5, or greater than 5. (When you think that you have got the program working correctly, try INPUTting a number of each type, e.g. 3, 5 and 7, to make sure it works correctly with all three.)

```
1Ø INPUT A
2Ø IF A > 5 THEN GOTO 5Ø
3Ø IF A = 5 THEN GOTO 6Ø
4Ø PRINT "YOUR NUMBER IS LESS THAN FIVE"
5Ø PRINT "YOUR NUMBER IS MORE THAN FIVE"
7Ø PRINT "YOUR NUMBER IS FIVE""
8Ø END
```

Program 3
This program asks you which year you were born, and which year it is now. It then takes one away from the other and tells you how old you are. (The answer will be one year out if you have not yet had your birthday this year.)

```
1Ø PRINT WHICH YEAR WERE YOU BORN?"
2Ø INPUT Y
3Ø PRINT WHICH YEAR IS IT THIS YEAR?"
4Ø INPUT Z
5Ø PRINT "YOU ARE; Y–Z; YEARS OLD"
6Ø END
```

Program 4
This program asks you for 5 numbers which it puts into an array A(1) to A(5). It then PRINTs all the locations of the array.

```
1Ø FOR R = 1 TO 5 STEP 5
2Ø INPUT A(R)
3Ø FOR S = 1 TO 5 STEP 1
4Ø PRINT A(S)
5Ø NEXT S
```

Program 5
This program READs DATA, two numbers at a time. It then divides the first number by the second number and PRINTs the answer. It then loops round and does the same thing again with the next two numbers until all the DATA has been read. It then PRINTs "I HAVE FINISHED".

```
1Ø DATA 6,4,8,Ø,1Ø,2,999
2Ø READ A,B
3Ø IF A = 999 THEN GOTO 6Ø
4Ø PRINT A/B
5Ø GOTO 2Ø
6Ø PRINT "I HAVE FINISHED"
7Ø END
```

Program 6
This program READs one piece of DATA at a time into memory box X, then PRINTs the value of X. When all the numbers in the DATA line have been read, the program RESTOREs the DATA and does the same thing again, so you should keep getting the numbers 1 to 8 PRINTed over and over again until you STOP or BREAK the program.

```
1Ø DATA 1,2,3,4,5,6,7,8,999
2Ø READ X
```

```
3∅ PRINT X;
4∅ GOTO 2∅
5∅ IF X = 999 THEN GOTO 6∅
6∅ RESTORE
```

Program 7

This program sets up an array and fills it with 40 RaNDom numbers between 1 and 1∅∅. All 40 numbers are then PRINTed. RUN the program and make a note on a piece of paper of the sixth number PRINTed. Then RUN the program again and ensure that the new sixth number is different from the one previously noted.

```
1∅ FOR R = 1 TO 4∅ STEP 1
2∅ LET A(R) = INT(RND(X) * 1∅∅) + 1
3∅ NEXT R
4∅ FOR S = 1 TO 4∅ STEP 1
5∅ PRINT A(S)
6∅ NEXT S
7∅ END
```

Program 8

This program calculates and PRINTs the values of G and H. Their correct values should be G = 7∅ and H = 2.

```
1∅ LET A = 1∅
2∅ LET B = 5
3∅ LET C = 2
4∅ LET D = 3
5∅ LET G = A * B + C
6∅ LET H = A/C + D
7∅ PRINT "G = ";G
8∅ PRINT "H = ";H
```

Program 9

This program sets up an array of 20 numbers and PRINTs them quickly in columns. The rest of the program then PRINTs out the numbers in exactly the same way but getting slower with each number PRINTed.

```
1∅ LET X = ∅
2∅ FOR R = 1 TO 2∅ STEP 1
3∅ LET A(R) = R
4∅ PRINT A(R),
5∅ NEXT R
6∅ FOR S = 1 TO 2∅ STEP 1
7∅ GOSUB 11∅
8∅ NEXT S
9∅ NEXT A
```

```
1ØØ END
11Ø LET X = X + 1ØØ
12Ø FOR T = 1 TO X STEP 1
13Ø NEXT T
14Ø PRINT A(S)
```

Program 10
This program will PRINT out each word, one on each line, but with
a delay between each PRINTed word.

```
1Ø PRINT "COMPUTING"
2Ø GOSUB 1ØØ
3Ø PRINT "IS"
4Ø GOSUB 1ØØ
5Ø PRINT "AN"
6Ø GOSUB 1ØØ
7Ø PRINT "INTERESTING"
8Ø GOSUB 1ØØ
9Ø PRINT "HOBBY"
1ØØ FOR R = 1 TO 1ØØØ STEP 1
11Ø NEXT R
12Ø RETURN
```

22

Some ideas for programs

You may be wondering what happens now that you have nearly finished reading this book. Well, one thing you ought to do is read Appendix 2. In that section you will find many useful facts about some of the keywords we have covered. They are improvements on the way you can use BASIC and most of them will make programming easier. Once you have read Appendix 2, we are certain that your programming will become even more enjoyable!

The next step you must take, if you have not already done so, is to begin writing your own programs. You probably have an idea or two in the back of your mind. If you haven't had time to think of anything to write, here are a few ideas you might like to consider.

1. It would be quite simple to get your computer to tell you how much foreign money you could exchange your pocket money for. This might be useful if you are going abroad for your holidays. The computer would need to ask you the exchange rate (you can get the exchange rate out of your daily paper), and multiply this by the amount of your pocket money.

For example, if you are going to Spain, and the paper tells you that the rate is 173 pesetas to the pound and your pocket money is 90 pence, the sum would look like this:

    LET P = 173 * ·9∅

P would then be the number of pesetas you would get. You could do lots of similar calculations for various amounts and take a list of them on holiday to help you.

2. You could find out the formula to convert Fahrenheit temperatures to Centigrade and write it into a program to help adults understand the different temperature scales. You could arrange for the computer to convert the other way round as well. Get the computer to ask which is the known temperature and work

out the other. Try to make the computer seem friendly in the way it asks for information.

3. A similar program could help you to convert litres to gallons. This could help car drivers in your family when buying petrol as more garages are using pumps which measure in litres rather than gallons.

A program similar to this would be of tremendous help in a supermarket when you want to know if a 375 gram box of Wheaty Crunch cornflakes costing 59 pence is better value than a 280 gram box costing 43 pence. Once programmed you could work out the best value for anything.

4. We have already had a program in an earlier chapter to help with tables. Perhaps you could write one to help you with spelling. Put the words into an ARRAY, then use a RaNDom number to choose one of the words. That word should then be displayed just long enough for you to read before it disappears off the top of the screen. Then INPUT your spelling of the word and get the computer to compare it with the correct spelling and be nice to you if you got it right. If not, perhaps this is the time for your computer to be not quite so nice! You can continue looping round, getting new words and keeping score until you always spell the words correctly. Spelling will never have been such fun.

5. If you know someone who does the football pools, you could write a program to help him or her win, by producing a list of RaNDom numbers. You could improve such a program as much as you liked. For instance, you could get the computer to check that each number it thinks of is different. You could also use the sorting routine to put them into numerical order to make it easier to fill out the coupon.

6. Have you got a piano or some other musical instrument? If so, you could get the computer to compose a tune for you! You could use just the white notes A to G, or you could get more ambitious and use the black notes as well. Get the computer to pick out the notes at random, then play the result and see what it sounds like. Horrible probably, but you never know, you may write a 'number

one' hit. You could get the computer to write two tunes, then get a friend to play the other one an octave apart. That would probably sound even worse, but you never know until you try!

7. Who do you know who owns a car? You could write a very useful program to tell them how many miles it does to a gallon of petrol. If you keep a record of the results over a long period you could get your screen to report when the car needs a tune-up, because it is not doing as many miles to the gallon as it used to.

These are only our ideas of programs that you might like to try to write. Perhaps you have better ideas with which to astonish your parents and friends. Never be put off because you feel your ideas are not good enough — go ahead and write the programs and you will find that new ideas will soon pop into your head.

23

More complicated programs

In this chapter you will find six programs which you should enjoy. Don't forget though, they can all be improved upon! We suggest that if you have not already done so, you now read the 'Variations and Tips on BASIC' that you will find in Appendix 2. You might find that you can use some of the tips in that section to make these programs a lot easier to enter.

Program 1 *** FOLLOW ME ***

```
1Ø PRINT "*** FOLLOW ME ***"
15 DIM S(1Ø)
2Ø PRINT "REPEAT THE NUMBERS"
3Ø PRINT "GIVEN BY THE COMPUTER."
4Ø FOR Q = 1 TO 1Ø STEP 1
5Ø LET S(Q) = INT (RND(X) * 4) + 1
55 REM RANDOM NUMBER FROM 1 TO 4
6Ø NEXT Q
7Ø FOR R = 1 TO 1Ø STEP 1
8Ø FOR V = 1 TO R STEP 1
85 PRINT
9Ø PRINT S(V),
1ØØ FOR W = 1 TO 4ØØ STEP 1
11Ø NEXT W
12Ø NEXT V
125 REM OPTIONALLY REPLACE LINES 13Ø, 14Ø, 15Ø WITH A
    CLEAR SCREEN STATEMENT
13Ø FOR X = 1 TO 40 STEP 1
14Ø PRINT
15Ø NEXT X
16Ø PRINT "REPEAT THE NUMBERS"
17Ø FOR Y = 1 TO R STEP 1
18Ø INPUT Z
```

```
19Ø IF Z <> S(Y) THEN GOTO 25Ø
2ØØ NEXT Y
21Ø NEXT R
22Ø PRINT "WELL DONE!"
225 PRINT
23Ø PRINT "ENTER AN X TO HAVE ANOTHER GO"
235 INPUT X$
24Ø GOTO 4Ø
25Ø PRINT
26Ø PRINT "SORRY, THE SEQUENCE WAS . . ."
27Ø FOR Q = 1 TO Y STEP 1
28Ø PRINT S(Q);"   ";
29Ø NEXT Q
295 PRINT
3ØØ GOTO 225
31Ø END
```

This program will display a number on the screen for a short time, which you must then repeat into the keyboard. Two numbers will then be displayed and then three, and so on up to ten. When repeating the numbers, remember to press the 'RETURN' key between each number. (If you want fewer than ten numbers change lines 4Ø and 7Ø. To change the speed with which the numbers are displayed, change line 1ØØ).

Program 2 *** MATCH IT ***
```
    5 DIM A(1Ø)
  1Ø PRINT "*** MATCH IT ***"
  4Ø LET G = Ø
  5Ø FOR Q = 1 TO 3 STEP 1
  6Ø LET A(Q) = INT(RND(X) * 9) + 1
  62 IF Q = 1 THEN GOTO 7Ø
  63 FOR T = 1 TO Q–1 STEP 1
  64 IF A(Q) = A(T) THEN GOTO 6Ø
  65 NEXT T
  70 NEXT Q
  75 PRINT "ENTER ØØØ TO GIVE UP"
  8Ø PRINT "ENTER GUESS  "; G + 1
  83 LET G = G + 1
  85 LET C = Ø
  86 LET A = Ø
  9Ø FOR Q = 4 TO 6 STEP 1
1ØØ INPUT A(Q)
1Ø5 IF A(Q) = ØØØ THEN GOTO 3ØØ
11Ø NEXT Q
12Ø FOR Q = 1 TO 3 STEP 1
```

```
13Ø IF A(Q) = A(Q + 3) THEN LET C = C + 1
14Ø IF A(Q) = A(Q + 3) THEN LET A = A − 1
15Ø FOR R = 4 TO 6 STEP 1
16Ø IF A(Q) = A(R) THEN LET A = A + 1
17Ø NEXT R
18Ø NEXT Q
2ØØ IF C = 3 THEN GOTO 27Ø
22Ø PRINT "CORRECT POSITIONS =   "; C;
23Ø PRINT "WRONG − ";A
25Ø PRINT
26Ø GOTO 8Ø
27Ø PRINT "ALL CORRECT IN  "; G; "  GUESSES"
28Ø GOTO 1Ø
3ØØ PRINT "THIS IS THE ANSWER"
31Ø FOR Z = 1 TO 3 STEP 1
32Ø PRINT A(Z); "   ";
33Ø NEXT Z
34Ø END
```

The computer will think of three numbers. You must work out what they are in the least number of tries possible. Remember to press 'RETURN' after each number.

Program 3   *** REVERSE ***

```
1Ø PRINT "*** REVERSE ***"
15 DIM A (1Ø)
16 DIM B (1Ø)
2Ø PRINT
25 FOR Q = 1 TO 9 STEP 1
3Ø LET A(Q)=INT (RND(X) * 9) + 1
5Ø IF Q = 1 THEN GOTO 9Ø
6Ø FOR R = 1 TO Q − 1 STEP 1
7Ø IF A(Q) = A(R) THEN GOTO 3Ø
8Ø NEXT R
9Ø NEXT Q
95 LET G = Ø
1ØØ PRINT "HOW MANY TO REVERSE? 1 TO 9"
11Ø FOR S = 1 TO 9 STEP 1
12Ø PRINT A(S);
13Ø NEXT S
15Ø INPUT P
16Ø IF P < 1 OR P > 9 THEN GOTO 15Ø
17Ø LET T = P
18Ø LET U = 1
19Ø LET B(U) = A(T)
2ØØ LET U = U + 1
```

```
21Ø LET T = T-1
22Ø IF T<>Ø THEN GOTO 19Ø
24Ø FOR Q = 1 TO P STEP 1
25Ø LET A(Q) = B(Q)
26Ø NEXT Q
27Ø LET G = G + 1
28Ø PRINT " TRY NUMBER "; G
29Ø PRINT
295 REM OPTIONAL CLEAR SCREEN
3ØØ GOTO 1ØØ
31Ø END
```

The computer will PRINT nine numbers which you must put into order in the least number of moves possible. You have to tell the computer to reverse the order of, say, the five leftmost numbers. For example, if the computer PRINTs

1 8 5 4 9 7 6 2 3

you would enter 5 to reverse the order of the first five numbers, which would give:

9 4 5 8 1 7 6 2 3

Now enter 9 to reverse all nine numbers which would give you:

3 2 6 7 1 8 5 4 9

This puts the '9' in the correct position. Now do the same with the '8', and so on, until all the numbers are in their correct places.

Program 4 *** HANGMAN ***
```
  5 DIM B$ (6)
 1Ø DIM C$ (4Ø)
 15 DIM W$ (6)
 2Ø PRINT "*** HANGMAN ***"
 25 PRINT
 3Ø LET W = Ø
 4Ø LET C = 1
 5Ø FOR P = 1 TO 6 STEP 1
 6Ø LET B$(P) = "*"
 7Ø NEXT P
 8Ø PRINT "ENTER A 6 LETTER WORD WITH A "
 9Ø PRINT "RETURN BETWEEN EACH LETTER"
1ØØ FOR Q = 1 TO 6 STEP 1
11Ø INPUT W$(Q)
12Ø NEXT Q
125 FOR S = 1 TO 4Ø STEP 1
```

90

```
128 REM OPTIONALLY REPLACE LINES 13Ø, 14Ø, 15Ø WITH
    A CLEAR SCREEN STATEMENT
13Ø FOR R = 1 TO 4Ø STEP 1
14Ø PRINT
15Ø NEXT R
17Ø PRINT
21Ø PRINT
22Ø FOR U = 1 TO 6 STEP 1
23Ø PRINT B$(U); "    ";
24Ø NEXT U
25Ø PRINT "GUESS THIS WORD"
255 PRINT
258 PRINT "ENTER A LETTER PLEASE"
259 IF W>7 THEN PRINT "OR ENTER 9 TO GIVE UP"
261 FOR T = 1 TO S STEP 1
262 PRINT C$(T); "    ";
263 NEXT T
264 PRINT
265 IF C = Ø THEN GOSUB 9ØØ
268 PRINT
27Ø INPUT C$(S)
275 IF C$(S) = "9" THEN GOTO 2ØØØ
28Ø LET C = Ø
29Ø FOR V = 1 TO 6 STEP 1
3ØØ IF C$(S) = W$(V) THEN LET B$(V) = C$(S)
31Ø IF C$(S) = W$(V) THEN LET C = 1
32Ø NEXT V
33Ø NEXT S
9ØØ LET W = W + 1
9Ø5 PRINT
9Ø6 REM TYPE SPACES IN PLACE OF THE DOTS
1ØØØ IF W > Ø THEN PRINT "= = = = ="
1Ø1Ø IF W = 2 THEN PRINT "/"
1Ø2Ø IF W > 2 THEN PRINT "/ . . . :"
1Ø3Ø IF W > 3 THEN PRINT " . . . . O"
1Ø4Ø IF W = 5 THEN PRINT " . . . I . I"
1Ø5Ø IF W = 6 THEN PRINT " . - - I . I"
1Ø6Ø IF W > 6 THEN PRINT " . - - I . I - -"
1Ø7Ø IF W > 4 THEN PRINT " . . . I . I"
1Ø8Ø IF W > 4 THEN PRINT " . . . - - -"
1Ø9Ø IF W = 8 THEN PRINT " . . . I"
11ØØ IF W = 8 THEN PRINT " . . . I"
111Ø IF W > 8 THEN PRINT " . . . I . I"
112Ø IF W > 8 THEN PRINT " . . . I . I"
113Ø RETURN
```

```
2000 PRINT "THE WORD IS . . ."
2005 PRINT
2010 FOR Z = 1 TO 6 STEP 1
2020 PRINT W$(Z);"   ";
2040 NEXT Z
2050 END
```

No problem with this one! You have to choose a six-letter word for a friend to guess. (You could put a space in as one of the letters to create a little confusion!) Remember to press RETURN after each letter, except for END which goes in as one word.

Program 5   *** RAFFLE DRAWER ***

```
10 PRINT "*** RAFFLE DRAWER ***"
12 LET T = 0
13 DIM N (10)
14 DIM P (10)
15 DIM C$ (10,6)
16 DIM N$ (10,6)
17 DIM F (10)
18 DIM L (10)
20 PRINT "ENTER THE NUMBER OF BOOKS SOLD"
30 INPUT B
40 FOR R = 1 TO B STEP 1
50 PRINT "ENTER COLOUR OF BOOK  "; R
60 INPUT C$(R)
70 PRINT "ENTER CODE NUMBER OF BOOK  "; R
80 INPUT N$(R)
90 PRINT "ENTER NUMBER OF FIRST TICKET"
95 PRINT "SOLD OUT OF BOOK  "; R
100 INPUT F(R)
110 PRINT "ENTER NUMBER OF LAST TICKET"
115 PRINT "SOLD OUT OF BOOK  "; R
120 INPUT L(R)
123 LET N(R) = L(R) − F(R) + 1
126 LET T = T + N(R)
130 NEXT R
140 PRINT "ENTER P AND PRESS RETURN"
150 PRINT "TO PICK A LUCKY TICKET"
160 INPUT Z$
162 REM OPTIONAL CLEAR SCREEN
165 PRINT
170 PRINT ". . . . . . WHICH IS . . . . . ."
180 PRINT
190 GOSUB 1000
200 LET X = INT (RND(X) * T) + 1
```

```
2Ø2 FOR S = 1 TO B STEP 1
2Ø3 IF X – N(S) > Ø THEN GOTO 2Ø6
2Ø5 GOTO 21Ø
2Ø6 LET X = X – N(S)
2Ø8 NEXT S
21Ø PRINT "ON A  "; C$(S) ;"  TICKET"
22Ø PRINT "SERIAL CODE NUMBER  "; N$(S)
23Ø GOSUB 1ØØØ
235 PRINT
24Ø PRINT "AND THE LUCKY NUMBER IS . . ."
25Ø PRINT
27Ø GOSUB 1ØØØ
276 LET X = X + F(S) – 1
28Ø PRINT "***  "; X;"  ***"
29Ø GOSUB 1ØØØ
3ØØ GOSUB 1ØØØ
31Ø PRINT
32Ø GOTO 14Ø
1ØØØ FOR R = 1 TO 1ØØØ STEP 1
1Ø1Ø NEXT R
1Ø2Ø RETURN
```

Another money-maker for your school. This raffle ticket prize-chooser is absolutely fair. It will allow you to have more than one book of raffle tickets for sale AND even two books with the same colour tickets. That is what the code number is for (the little number which appears on the bottom of each ticket). Just make sure that you sell the tickets in sequence, and don't buy any yourself, or someone will shout 'fiddle' if you win!

Program 6   *** BINGO CALLER ***

```
1Ø PRINT "*** BINGO CALLER ***"
2Ø DIM A (9Ø)
25 DIM B (9Ø)
3Ø GOTO 2ØØØ
4Ø FOR Q = 1 TO 7Ø STEP 1
5Ø LET A(Q) = INT (RND(X) * 9Ø) + 1
6Ø IF Q = 1 THEN GOTO 1ØØ
7Ø FOR R = 1 TO Q – 1 STEP 1
8Ø  IF A(Q) = A(R) THEN GOTO 5Ø
9Ø NEXT R
1ØØ NEXT Q
11Ø FOR S = 1 TO 9Ø STEP 1
115 PRINT
12Ø PRINT "PRESS P AND RETURN"
13Ø INPUT P$
```

```
135 REM OPTIONAL CLEAR SCREEN
140 IF P$ = "CHECK" THEN GOTO 2500
145 FOR R = 1 TO 10 STEP 1
146 PRINT
147 NEXT R
148 LET Z = A(S)
150 GOTO 1000
160 PRINT
165 PRINT A(S)
180 LET B(Z) = Z
190 NEXT S
200 END
1000 IF Z = 10 THEN PRINT "10 — DOWNING STREET"
1020 IF Z = 90 THEN PRINT "90 — TOP OF THE HOUSE"
1030 IF Z = 10 OR Z = 90 THEN GOTO 160
1040 IF Z/10 = INT(Z/10) THEN PRINT "BLIND "; Z
1050 IF Z = 1 THEN PRINT "1 — KELLYS EYE"
1060 IF Z = 2 THEN PRINT "2 — ONE LITTLE DUCK"
1070 IF Z = 4 THEN PRINT "4 — KNOCK AT THE DOOR"
1080 IF Z = 8 THEN PRINT "8 — GARDEN GATE"
1090 IF Z = 9 THEN PRINT "9 — DOCTORS ORDERS"
1100 IF Z = 11 THEN PRINT "11 — LEGS ELEVEN"
1110 IF Z = 12 THEN PRINT "12 — ONE DOZEN"
1120 IF Z = 13 THEN PRINT "13 — UNLUCKY FOR SOME"
1130 IF Z = 16 THEN PRINT "16 — SWEET SIXTEEN"
1140 IF Z = 21 THEN PRINT "21 — KEY OF THE DOOR"
1150 IF Z = 22 THEN PRINT "22 — TWO LITTLE DUCKS"
1160 IF Z = 26 THEN PRINT "26 — BED AND BREAKFAST"
1170 IF Z = 45 THEN PRINT "45 — HALF-WAY THERE"
1180 IF Z = 65 THEN PRINT "65 — OLD AGE PENSION"
```

```
1190 IF Z = 66 THEN PRINT "66 — CLICKETY CLICK"
1200 IF Z = 69 THEN PRINT "69 — BRIGHTON LINE"
1210 IF Z = 76 THEN PRINT "76 — WAS SHE WORTH IT?"
1220 IF Z = 88 THEN PRINT "88 — TWO FAT LADIES"
1230 IF Z = 33 THEN PRINT "33 — ALL THE THREES"
1240 IF Z = 44 THEN PRINT "44 — ALL THE FOURS"
1250 IF Z = 55 THEN PRINT "55 — ALL THE FIVES"
1260 IF Z = 77 THEN PRINT "77 — ALL THE SEVENS"
1990 GOTO 160
2000 PRINT "DO YOU WANT INSTRUCTIONS? Y OR N"
2010 INPUT P$
2030 IF P$ <> "Y" THEN GOTO 2080
2040 PRINT "TO PICK OUT A NUMBER PRESS"
2050 PRINT "P AND THEN RETURN"
2060 PRINT
2070 PRINT "TO CHECK THE NUMBERS ALREADY"
2075 PRINT "CALLED OUT ENTER CHECK"
2080 PRINT
2090 PRINT "THE MACHINE TAKES SOME TIME"
2100 PRINT "TO SORT OUT THE NUMBERS, SO"
2110 PRINT "PLEASE BE PATIENT"
2120 GOTO 40
2500 FOR V = 1 TO S−1 STEP 1
2510 IF A(V) = 0 THEN GOTO 2530
2520 PRINT A(V),
2530 NEXT V
2540 PRINT
2550 PRINT "ENTER C TO CONTINUE CALLING"
2560 PRINT "ENTER B TO BEGIN A NEW GAME"
2570 INPUT P$
2580 IF P$ = "C" THEN GOTO 120
2590 IF P$ = "B" THEN GOTO 40
2600 GOTO 2550
2610 END
```

Another fund raising program for school. If you wanted to make the program shorter, you could leave out the instructions by deleting line 30, and lines 2000 to 2120. You could also leave out line 150, and 1000 to 1990 if you did not want the 'clickety click' type words.

After someone calls BINGO you can check on all the numbers called, and the last number PRINTed will be the last one called. If that person made a mistake, and hasn't won, just type 'C' to continue getting numbers.

Certain computers have a 'FAST' and 'SLOW' option. If your

computer is one of these, and the program runs very slowly, we suggest you add the following statement lines:

```
35 FAST
1Ø5 SLOW
```

As we said before, it is up to you to experiment with these programs. The more you do so the better at programming you will become.

Good Luck
and Happy Programming
David Parker and Martin Hann.

Appendix 1

Suggested solutions to problems set in Chapter 21

Please note that:

(a) Your computer will have advised you of syntax errors, either at the time of entering each program line or during the RUNning of the program.

(b) You may never be aware that logic errors exist in a program if you do not check and test your program properly. We suggest that you attempt to test every conceivable INPUT and possibility before showing a new program to your parents or to a friend. There is nothing more embarrassing than the moment when your latest pride and joy throws up an impossible answer or does something unexpected.

Here are our suggested answers to the 'bugs' in Chapter 21:

Program 1
Line 3∅ should be: 3∅ PRINT B
Comment: The variable B should not be inside quotation marks. This is a logic error.

Program 2
Line 3∅ should read:

    3∅ IF A = 5 THEN GOTO 7∅

Two lines are needed at 45 and 55:

    45 GOTO 1∅
    55 GOTO 1∅

Comments: Line 3∅ attempts to go to a line that does not exist. This is both a logic error and a syntax error.

If a program seems to go mad and PRINTs out far more than you would expect it to, it is probably because you have left out a GOTO or END statement. These would be logic errors.

Program 3
Line 1Ø should be:

   1Ø PRINT "WHICH YEAR WERE YOU BORN?"

Line 3Ø should be:

   3Ø PRINT "WHICH YEAR IS IT THIS YEAR?"

Line 5Ø should be:

   5Ø PRINT "YOU ARE   "; Z − Y; " YEARS OLD"

Comments: Both lines 1Ø and 3Ø require quotation marks before the word WHICH. These are syntax errors. Line 5Ø has three errors. Quotation marks are missing both after the word ARE and before the word YEARS. These are syntax errors. There is also a logic error; did you notice that our program gave a minus number?

Program 4
Line 1Ø should be:

   1Ø FOR R = 1 TO 5 STEP 1

Another line is required at line 25:

   25 NEXT R

Comments: The error at line 1Ø is a logic error. Line 25 is required to complete the FOR NEXT loop.

Program 5
Line 1Ø is incomplete:

   1Ø DATA 6, 4, 8, Ø, 1Ø, 2, 999, 999

Comments: Line 2Ø needs to READ two items of DATA each time or else the program will give an OUT OF DATA syntax error. Division by zero (the fourth item of DATA) is not allowed by computers and will 'crash' your program (stop it RUNning). To prevent this happening in a future program, add the following line just before where your program may encounter such an attempt to divide by zero:

   35 IF B = Ø THEN GOTO 1ØØ
   1ØØ PRINT "ATTEMPTED DIVISION BY ZERO"
   11Ø PRINT "CALL FOR PROGRAMMING HELP"
   12Ø END

   If the calculation is not too important you could change line 12Ø to read:

   12Ø GOTO 2Ø

and allow the program to continue after having given the PRINTed message at lines 1∅∅ and 11∅.

Program 6
Change line 5∅ to:

    25 IF X = 999 THEN GOTO 6∅

Also add line 7∅ as follows:

    7∅ GOTO 1∅

Comments: The first four lines of the program will READ and PRINT the DATA (including 999) and will then produce an OUT OF DATA error. This is remedied by changing line 5∅. These changes will allow the first PRINT of 1 to 8, but will not continually repeat the cycle without the 7∅ GOTO 1∅ statement.

Program 7
Add these lines:

    5 DIM A (4∅)
    6 RANDOMIZE (perhaps)

Change line 5∅ to read:

    5∅ PRINT A(S); or 5∅ PRINT A(S),

Comments: Line 5 is a syntax error. Always put DIM statements at the very beginning of your programs. This ensures that the ARRAY is DIMensioned before you attempt to use it. It is possible to get a DOUBLE DIMENSIONED error which can occur if:
(a) You attempt to DIMension an array of 10 or fewer locations (the computer will automatically DIMension 10 locations unless you tell it to provide more).
(b) Your program has a GOTO statement which goes back to a DIMension statement a second time (putting DIMs at the head of your programs should help to stop this happening).
   Line 5∅ is a logic error. It may be very difficult to read the sixth number PRINTed because of the speed it goes off the top of the screen! The addition of the comma or the semicolon solves this problem. Line 6 may not be an error; it depends upon how your computer deals with RaNDom numbers. This would be a logic error.

Program 8
Change line 5∅ to read:

    5∅ LET G = A * (B + C)

Change line 6∅ to read:

    6∅ LET H = A/(C + D)

Comments: If you write a program which works its maths out incorrectly, that would be a logic error. Remember that brackets change the usual order in which the computer does its calculations. Always check your program with test data and a calculator.

Program 9

Add: 2 DIM A (2∅)
Change: 14∅ PRINT A(S),
Add: 15∅ RETURN
Delete 9∅

Comments: Line 2 is needed for the same reason as line 5 in program 7 was needed. Line 14∅ is a logic error. The comma tells the computer to PRINT in columns across the screen. The subroutine which starts at line 11∅ must have a RETURN statement. In this program, line 9∅ is not required at all, which is why you would have got a NEXT WITHOUT FOR syntax error message. If you get a NEXT WITHOUT FOR error, the problem is often a good bit earlier in the program than the line number in the error message would have you believe. The error can often be traced to your program having been sent into the middle of a FOR NEXT loop in error.

Program 10

Add: 95 END

Comments: The program will RUN correctly until it reaches line 9∅ at which point it will continue into the subroutine until it gets to line 12∅ when it will give a RETURN WITHOUT GOSUB syntax error message. As the program did not arrive at line 1∅∅ via a GOSUB statement, the computer had no note of a line number to RETURN to when it got to line 12∅. Always separate your main programs and subroutines with an END or GOTO statement which will prevent the computer from running into a following subroutine.

Appendix 2

Variations and tips on BASIC

Throughout this book we have made every effort to ensure that the programs and exercises can be RUN on most computers that support the BASIC language. This was not easy because, as with spoken English, different words may mean different things depending upon where the language is spoken. For instance, a word in Scotland may not have the same meaning as the same word in America. Also, a small child will not know as many words as an adult.

This also happens with BASIC, where a word used in one computer may do something slightly different in another computer. Also, a computer with just a small BASIC language will not have as many words available to it as one with a larger BASIC language.

This appendix is divided into two sections. Section 1 describes some variations in the keywords that we have used in this book. We suggest that you experiment with the changes we describe as many BASICs will allow some, if not all, of these variations. Section 2 describes a few BASIC words which are available to many machines, but which we have not attempted to describe in this book. Once you have mastered those in this book you will find it very easy to learn these new features and to use them in your programs.

Section 1

DATA Works with READ and RESTORE and is not available on some machines. If yours is one of these, Chapter 18 will explain how to get round this. Also, if you SAVE the program in Chapter 18 and then LOAD it again, you may find all the 'rude words' and names are still available for use if you type GOTO 17∅ instead of RUN. Try it; it may work on your computer if it doesn't support DATA.

END   Many computers need the last program statement to be an END statement. On other computers it may not be necessary. What does yours need?

FOR   This works with TO, STEP and NEXT. Many computers do not need the word STEP if the increase is by one each time. Some computers insist on passing through a FOR NEXT loop at least once, even if it looks as though your program doesn't tell it to! Also if you have, say, a FOR NEXT loop FOR R = 1 TO 5, when the computer gets out of the loop R will equal 6! So be careful if you use R again later without doing a LET R statement to set it to 5 (or whatever you want it to be). Most computers do not need a letter after the NEXT statement as the computer often works out the correct FOR line number by itself. See if this little routine will work in your computer:

```
2∅ FOR R = 1 TO 5
3∅ PRINT R
4∅ NEXT
5∅ PRINT "AFTER THE LOOPING, R =   "; R
```

GOSUB   Most computers will only allow a line number after the GOSUB, but some will allow a variable:

```
4∅ LET T = 5∅∅∅
5∅ GOSUB T
```

GOTO   See notes on GOSUB above.

INPUT   Study these two routines. They both do exactly the same, but the second is much shorter:

```
One:     3∅ PRINT "ENTER A NUMBER"
         4∅ INPUT N
Two:     3∅ INPUT "ENTER A NUMBER  "; N
```

Do you see that we have done away with 'PRINT' in line 3∅ and used INPUT? Also, variable N is now on the same line following a semicolon. Many computers allow this — try it on yours. If, when you use the INPUT statement, your computer doesn't leave a copy of what you INPUT, use a PRINT statement directly after the INPUT statement to PRINT out the variable.

LET   Most machines do not insist on using LET in a line. Try this:

```
1∅ A = 5
2∅ B = 7
3∅ C = A + B
4∅ PRINT C
```

LIST   Some machines allow variations. Try:

LIST	lists the whole program
LIST 1∅∅	lists just line 1∅∅
LIST −1∅∅	lists all lines up to 1∅∅
LIST 1∅∅−	lists all lines after 1∅∅
LIST 1∅∅−2∅∅	lists all lines between 1∅∅ and 2∅∅.

LOAD As each machine appears to have its own set of rules regarding LOAD and SAVE, we can only suggest that you read your own computer's manual very carefully to ensure that you get the most out of this important feature.

NEXT See FOR above.

PRINT Try using a question mark (?) instead of typing PRINT:

    1∅ A = 5
    2∅?A

If this works, try LISTing your program and you will see that the computer has spelt the word PRINT out in full for you.

RANDOM Also **RANDOMISE** and **RANDOMIZE** Because of the many variations between one machine and the next we can only suggest that you read your own computer's manual on the subject.

READ   See *DATA*.

RESTORE See *DATA*.

RND   See *RANDOM*.

SAVE   See *LOAD*.

STEP   See *FOR*.

  Here are the last few tips to see you on your way:
(a) Some computers will allow you to put several different statements on one line like this:

    1∅ A = 5: B = 6: C = A + B:?C

As you can see, each statement is separated by a colon. (Some computers need a backslash\). This feature is very useful as it reduces the time it takes to enter a program into the computer. LOADing and SAVEing are also much quicker.
(b) It is not necessary to leave spaces between the letters, numbers and statements on a line. Look at this:

    1∅A = 5:B = 6:C = A + B:?C

Once again, it is quicker to LOAD, SAVE and enter programs like this. Also the program will not take up so much of the computer's memory. Many people, however, say that it is much more difficult to read such programs. What do you think?

(c) We have assumed that the usual screen width of a computer is 32 characters. There are many computers that can PRINT 40, 48, 64 or even 80 characters on one line. If you are lucky enough to have one of these you will be able to combine some of the PRINT lines in our programs on to one line.

(d) If your computer has the keywords CLS or HOME then you will be able to substitute these simple instructions for the Clear Screen routines described and used in various places in this book.

Section 2

In this section we have listed a few of the BASIC words that we have not attempted to cover in this book. Once you have mastered our book you will be able to program most of the things that you would like to do. This section shows you that there is, however, more to learn if you want to. There are several good books available and some of them are listed in Appendix 3.

LEN	SQR	GET
LEFT$	TAN	NOT
RIGHT$	**	PRINT AT
MID$	↑	PRINT USING
CHR$	PEEK	PRINT%
CODE	POKE	OPEN
ASC	USR	CLOSE
SIN	MAT	ON GOSUB
ABS	MAT READ	ON GOTO
VTAB	HTAB	SLOW
FAST	ON ERROR	

Appendix 3

Further Reading

1. **ZX81 BASIC Book** by Robin Norman. Newnes Technical Books, Borough Green, Sevenoaks, Kent TN15 8PH.
2. **Learning BASIC with your Sinclair ZX80** by Robin Norman. Newnes Technical Books, Borough Green, Sevenoaks, Kent TN15 8PH.
3. **Beginner's Guide to BASIC Programming** by A. P. Stephenson. Newnes Technical Books, Borough Green, Sevenoaks, Kent TN15 8PH.
4. **BASIC BASIC** by James S. Coan. Hayden Book Co. Inc., Rochelle Park, New Jersey, U.S.A.
5. **Illustrating BASIC** by Donald Alcock. Cambridge University Press, Cambridge.
6. **Learning BASIC Fast** by Claude DeRossi. Reston Publishing Co. Inc., Reston, Virginia, U.S.A.
7. **Fred Learns About Computers** Published by MacDonald and Evans, Plymouth.
8. **The Computer** by David Carey. Ladybird Books, Loughborough.
9. **Computer Programming in BASIC** by L. R. Carter and E. Huzan. (Teach Yourself Books) Hodder and Stoughton, London.

Appendix 4

Glossary

Alpha Short for alphabetical; the letters of the alphabet.

Alphanumeric or **String Variable** A variable which can contain any character accessible via the keyboard.

Array A memory box divided into separate memory locations.

BASIC Short for Beginners All-purpose Symbolic Instruction Code. A 'high-level' computer language which is especially suitable for small computers. It was originally intended for beginners but is now one of the most widely used computer languages in the world.

Binary Number A number represented by 1s and 0s, which is how the computer remembers and works with numbers. A binary number is usually eight bits (one byte) long; for example, 00000101 is 5, and 00101001 is 41.

Bit The smallest part of a computer's memory. It is, in effect, a switch which can be set to 'on' (a 1) or 'off' (a zero).

Bug An error in a program.

Byte Eight bits.

Character A single letter or number, or a symbol of some sort; e.g. A, B, 4, +, *.

Condition A fact which may be true or untrue.

Conditional Jump An instruction to go to another part of a program only if a certain condition is true.

Crash When a program stops running because of an error.

Debugging Finding and correcting bugs in programs.

Disk A circular piece of plastic coated with a magnetic substance, used for recording programs or data.

Disk Drive Machine which holds disk(s) and reads or writes programs or data on them.

Edit To change part of a program.

Enter To put statement lines or data into the computer by pressing

106

the RETURN (or NEWLINE or ENTER) key on the keyboard.

Error Code A message consisting of numbers or letters to tell you an error has occurred, and what type of error it is.

Exponential Notation A short way of showing very large numbers. A letter 'E' within a number shows it is an exponent, then another number to the right of the 'E' tells you how many places the decimal point must be moved to arrive at the true figure, e.g. $4.56E+10 = 45,6\emptyset\emptyset,\emptyset\emptyset\emptyset,\emptyset\emptyset\emptyset$.

Flowchart A chart showing the order in which parts of a program are to be performed, and how the computer is to work out the solution to a problem. Used to work out how a program should be written to achieve the desired result.

Hardware The physical parts of a computer system; the computer, terminals, printers, disk drives, etc.

High-level Language A programming language such as BASIC, which uses English-like words to instruct the computer.

Integer A whole number.

Integer BASIC A type of BASIC which works only in whole numbers.

K 1024 bytes of memory.

Keyword A word of instruction to the computer.

Literal A character or characters within quotes which is stored exactly as it is written (literally) by the computer.

Load To put a program into the computer's memory from a separate storage device such as a cassette recorder or disk drive.

Logic The reasoning behind what the computer is told to do.

Logic Error A mistake in telling the computer what to do.

Loop A set of statement lines which are performed over and over again.

Low-level Language Programming language which is written in machine code, or something very close to it.

Machine Code The computer's own language.

Numeric Having to do with numbers; any number.

Numeric Variable A variable which can be given a numeric value.

Priority The order in which the computer does its arithmetic.

Program The complete list of instructions which the computer performs in order to solve a problem.

Random Number A number picked out by chance.

Read and Write memory — 'RAM' Memory which can be used for storing programs and for doing calculations, etc.

Read-Only Memory — 'ROM' Instructions held in the computer's memory and usually written in machine code. These are used by the computer to interpret keywords and other input from the keyboard, etc.

Routine See subroutine.

Save To store programs or data on a separate storage device such as a cassette or disk.

Software Computer programs.

Statement An instruction to the computer.

Storage Any part of a computer or recording device which can store programs or data.

String A character or characters stored in an alphanumeric variable.

String Variable See alphanumeric variable.

Subroutine A sequence of computer statements which, although only part of a complete computer program, will nevertheless function by itself. Often used more than once during a run of a computer program by means of GOSUB instructions.

Subscript A letter or number following a memory box name which identifies a particular memory location, usually part of an array.

Syntax The way in which an instruction to the computer is worded.

Syntax Error A mistake in the way an instruction is written.

System The complete set of hardware and software which together perform the required processing operations.

Terminal A device, usually consisting of a video screen and keyboard, used to communicate with the computer.

Value The quantity that a variable represents.

Variable A symbol that can represent letters or numbers or other characters. See alphanumeric variable and numeric variable.

Index